D1496376

Palgrave Studies in Victims and Victimology

Series Editors
Matthew Hall
University of Lincoln
Lincoln, UK

Pamela Davies
Department of Social Sciences
Northumbria University
Newcastle upon Tyne, UK

In recent decades, a growing emphasis on meeting the needs and rights of victims of crime in criminal justice policy and practice has fuelled the development of research, theory, policy and practice outcomes stretching across the globe. This growth of interest in the victim of crime has seen victimology move from being a distinct subset of criminology in academia to a specialist area of study and research in its own right.

Palgrave Studies in Victims and Victimology showcases the work of contemporary scholars of victimological research and publishes some of the highest-quality research in the field. The series reflects the range and depth of research and scholarship in this burgeoning area, combining contributions from both established scholars who have helped to shape the field and more recent entrants. It also reflects both the global nature of many of the issues surrounding justice for victims of crime and social harm and the international span of scholarship researching and writing about them.

Editorial Board
Antony Pemberton, Tilburg University, Netherlands
Jo-Anne Wemmers, Montreal University, Canada
Joanna Shapland, Sheffield University, UK
Jonathan Doak, Durham University, UK

More information about this series at
http://www.palgrave.com/gp/series/14571

Marianne Inéz Lien • Jørgen Lorentzen

Men's Experiences of Violence in Intimate Relationships

palgrave
macmillan

DISCARD
WLU BRANTFORD CAMPUS

Marianne Inéz Lien
University of Oslo
Blindern, Oslo, Norway

Jørgen Lorentzen
Hedda Foundation
Nesodden, Norway

Palgrave Studies in Victims and Victimology
ISBN 978-3-030-03993-6   ISBN 978-3-030-03994-3   (eBook)
https://doi.org/10.1007/978-3-030-03994-3

Library of Congress Control Number: 2018962558

© The Editor(s) (if applicable) and The Author(s) 2019 This book is an open access publication
Open Access This book is licensed under the terms of the Creative Commons Attribution 4.0
International License (http://creativecommons.org/licenses/by/4.0/), which permits use, sharing, adaptation, distribution and reproduction in any medium or format, as long as you give appropriate credit to
the original author(s) and the source, provide a link to the Creative Commons licence and indicate if
changes were made.
The images or other third party material in this book are included in the book's Creative Commons
licence, unless indicated otherwise in a credit line to the material. If material is not included in the book's
Creative Commons licence and your intended use is not permitted by statutory regulation or exceeds the
permitted use, you will need to obtain permission directly from the copyright holder.
The use of general descriptive names, registered names, trademarks, service marks, etc. in this publication
does not imply, even in the absence of a specific statement, that such names are exempt from the relevant
protective laws and regulations and therefore free for general use.
The publisher, the authors and the editors are safe to assume that the advice and information in this book
are believed to be true and accurate at the date of publication. Neither the publisher nor the authors or
the editors give a warranty, express or implied, with respect to the material contained herein or for any
errors or omissions that may have been made. The publisher remains neutral with regard to jurisdictional
claims in published maps and institutional affiliations.

Cover illustration: © Francesco Carta fotografo / Getty Images

This Palgrave Macmillan imprint is published by the registered company Springer Nature Switzerland AG
The registered company address is: Gewerbestrasse 11, 6330 Cham, Switzerland

Preface

This book is based on a three-part study of violence against men in intimate relationships in Norway. Funded by the Det norske Barne-, ungdoms- og familiedirektoratet, Bufdir (Norway's Children Youth and Family Directorate), the study was conducted by researchers Marianne Inéz Lien (University of Oslo) and Jørgen Lorentzen (The Hedda Foundation and Claes Ekenstam, Borås University), in collaboration with Proba Research. The study includes a literature review of Nordic prevalence studies of violence against men over the age of 18; a survey of public awareness of the prevalence of violence against men and the help available; and a qualitative interview study of men who have experienced various forms of violence in close relationships. The interviewees were all current or former users of the Norwegian family protection office, crisis centres and centres for incest and sexual abuse.

In writing this book, Marianne Inéz Lien and Jørgen Lorentzen have edited the original Norwegian study substantially. We have removed sections dealing with the Norwegian support services, as well as most of both the quantitative research section and the literature review. This is because international readers are either likely to be familiar with the majority of this information, or it is of less interest in an international context. The emphasis and focus of this book are therefore on the qualitative aspect of the study, since this contains those findings which are most interesting and which offer new insights and understanding into violence in intimate relationships in an international perspective.

We would like to thank all those who contributed to this project. In particular, we would like to thank Claes Ekenstam for the interviews with the men who have suffered sexual abuse (incest). Special thanks also go to our colleagues in Proba Research: Pia Dybvik Staalesen, for conducting the survey, and Trude Torbjørnsrud, who implemented the quality control for the Norwegian report. Thanks also go to the senior advisor for the Department for the Prevention of Violence (Bufdir), Elin Skogøy, Elise Skarsaune and the rest of the team for their exceptional support and contributions to our work during this project. We would also like to thank the following: the peer review group for their feedback when we presented our preliminary results and analyses, as well as their comments on the draft report; Arnfinn Andersen at the Norwegian Centre for Violence and Traumatic Stress Studies (Norsk kompetansesenter for vold og traumatisk stress) for his valuable comments during our work on this book; and the staff at the Humanities and Social Science Libraries at the University of Oslo for their contribution to the project and encouragement.

We are also extremely grateful to our translator, Deborah Dawkin, for her skill, dedication and attention to detail in the translation of this book. We would also like to thank Josie Taylor and Poppy Hull for their outstanding editorial support. Thank you for your patience and for bringing this book forward.

Last but not least, a big thank-you goes to all the men who participated in this project, sharing their experiences and knowledge of violence in intimate relationships. Thank you for your willingness to share these very difficult experiences with us.

Oslo, Norway   Marianne Inéz Lien
Nesodden, Norway   Jørgen Lorentzen

Contents

List of Figures

1

Violence Against Men in Intimate Relationships

It is a common assumption that men are only exposed to violence in the public space, while women are exposed to violence in intimate relationships. We regularly read about "mindless" or "gratuitous" violence, in which men are both the victims and the perpetrators. Such violence generally takes place in public spaces. In the last few decades we have become increasingly aware of the violence inflicted on women and children behind closed doors, in our homes. It is the violence that takes place within intimate relationships which has been the main subject of research in Norway and internationally—which in a host of countries has, in part, prompted the provision of help and intervention.

Recent research in Norway, based on various quantitative studies in which both women and men have been asked the same questions, has led to an increasing focus on violence in families and other intimate relationships which also affects a large number of men (Pape and Stefansen 2004; Haaland et al. 2005; Sogn and Hjemdal 2009; Thoresen and Hjemdal 2014). Despite this, violence towards men in intimate relationships is a relatively unexplored field in the Nordic context. In particular, research is severely lacking on the experiences of men who are the victims of violence in intimate relationships, and the help they might need. This book

© The Author(s) 2019
M. I. Lien, J. Lorentzen, *Men's Experiences of Violence in Intimate Relationships*,
Palgrave Studies in Victims and Victimology,
https://doi.org/10.1007/978-3-030-03994-3_1

1

aims, in some small way, to fill this gap in our knowledge. In international research there are few narrative studies on male victims of partner violence (Allen-Collinson 2009a, b; Corbally 2015).

There has been some conflict in international research (and international debate around domestic violence) between those who claim gender symmetry—that violence is more or less equally distributed between women and men—and those who believe that domestic violence is almost wholly a question of men's violence against women (Archer 2002; Kimmel 2002; Dobash and Dobash 2004). Much of this discussion is based on statistical analysis of domestic violence. We do not aim, therefore, to engage in this debate directly, since our analysis is a more phenomenological analysis of men's experiences of being subjected to violence and their help-seeking.

Aims and Objectives

This book is dived into three sections: a summary of prevalence studies; a survey; and qualitative research interviews. The latter sub-study comprises the main body of this book and includes three separate interview studies.

This book has two overarching objectives. First, we want to give men themselves the greatest space possible to tell their stories. Many people will find it improbable, or hard to understand, that a man might be subjected to systematic and serious violence from a female partner. The idea that a woman may be the aggressor, rather than the caregiver, can be counter-intuitive and stands in opposition to social norms of femininity (Richardson 2005). This book takes as its point of departure that violence and gender must be empirically investigated rather than assumed in studies of violence. It has therefore been important for us to offer quite detailed descriptions of events and experiences of violence, not because the experiences of violence inflicted on men differ enormously from those of women who are similarly exposed, but because we are generally unused to this switch in gender. Secondly, we will investigate the new empirical evidence about violence against men in intimate relationships, and look at ways in which this can bring greater nuance and a wider understanding to the more established theories of violence in intimate relationships.

The questions that form the basis of this study are as follows:

- What do prevalence studies from the Nordic countries tell us about the vulnerability of men, the characteristics of the violence, the relationships in which violence takes place, its consequences and the help available?
- How do men experience being subjected to violence in intimate relationships?
- What kinds of help do these men require?
- Of those men who have sought and received help, what are their experiences?
- Is there public awareness of the help available to men?
- Can new empirical research about men bring a more nuanced and wider understanding to the more established theories of violence in intimate relationships?

The project comprises three sub-studies that aim to address these questions. The first of these is a literature study of Nordic prevalence studies of violence against men in intimate relationships.

The second consists of a questionnaire about awareness among the Norwegian public about the help that is available, including crisis centres, family protection offices and centres against incest and sexual assault, and the level of awareness that these are (also) available to men. The questionnaire further includes a survey of whether the male respondents who had been subject to violence in intimate relationships had sought help, and, if not, why this was the case.

It is important to note that services offered in Norway for men experiencing violence in intimate relationships are relatively unusual. There are 19 centres for victims of incest which have, since their inception in the 1970s, treated both men and women who have experienced sexual abuse within or outside the family. There are also 40 crisis centres, which were originally traditional crisis centres for women, similar to those in various other countries, but which opened their doors to men in 2010. In 2010 the government introduced a new a gender-neutral law in relation to crisis centres, making it mandatory for local councils to offer services to men and women on an equal basis. Since then, the proportion of men at crisis centres has steadily increased.

In the third sub-study we interviewed 28 male victims about their experiences of violence within intimate relationships. Here our focus is on the kinds of relationship in which violence takes place and the consequences of that violence on these men, both now and in the past. We also investigate the experiences of men who have received help. In particular, we have been concerned with the experiences they have with the family protection service, crisis centres and centres against incest and sexual assault.

Based on the information gathered from these three sub-studies, we discuss how a greater understanding of violence against men in intimate relationships can help challenge and further develop established theories of violence in intimate relationships. Finally, we offer recommendations for possible improvements to existing services offered to men exposed to violence in intimate relationships, including sexual abuse.

What Is Violence in Intimate Relationships?

The World Health Organization (WHO) defines violence as "the intentional use of physical force or power, threatened or actual, against oneself, another person, or against a group or community, that either results in or has a high likelihood of resulting in injury, death, psychological harm, maldevelopment, or deprivation." The use of physical force or power also includes neglect and all forms of physical, sexual and psychological abuse (Krug 2002, p. 5). The Norwegian therapist and scholar Per Isdal's definition goes further in defining the effects of violence on the victim: "Violence is any act directed at another person which causes injury, pain, fear or humiliation, thereby causing the other person to do something against their will, or to refrain from doing something they want" (Isdal 2000, p. 18).

The most concrete way to identify a violent act is to define various forms of violence. Isdal (2000) suggests that the following forms of violence are the most relevant when researching violence in intimate relationships:

- Sexual violence: all violence that involves sexual acts or sexual approaches (sexual harassment/violation, abuse, rape).
- Physical violence: violence involving physical contact (kicking, hitting, pulling, biting, etc.).
- Psychological violence: verbal or similar violence that frightens and harms others (threats, humiliation, controlling others, isolating others, etc.).
- Latent violence: violence that works by virtue of its possibility. Having experienced violence means that one knows that can happen again. Violence is then present by virtue of its possibility, and it controls others through mood/temper, tone of voice, how a door is opened, the way someone leaves, etc. The risk of further violence can control everything the victim does without any actively aggressive behaviour.
- Material violence: violence against inanimate objects (breaking objects, destroying things that matter to others, etc.).
- Economic violence: control of another person's financial resources or economy.

In this book we have chosen to capture a wide spectrum of men's experiences of violence, in which all of the above-mentioned elements are included. Most books on violence in intimate relationships do not discuss sexual abuse. We have however chosen to include this, and have interviewed men about their experiences both as children and as adults. This is because sexual violence against men is under-communicated, these men are often subject to multiple victimisation, and we wanted to throw light on the need of these men for help. Most sexual abuse of men is perpetrated by members of their families or others who are close, often in relationships of trust (see Chap. 6). We have additionally included and looked at the threat of being denied contact with their own children/ sabotage of that contact, as well as pressure and coercion from families, including honour-related violence.

In this book, violence in *intimate relationships* is understood to mean violence or threats of violence within couples, families, including the wider family, friendships and other relationships of trust or dependence.

Contemporary Theoretical Debates on Violence in Intimate Relationships

Both Nordic and international studies on violence in intimate relationships have generally focused on the violence of men against women and children within the family. Over the years a number of different terms have been used when referring to this violence in these studies: *wife abuse, wife battering, family violence, domestic violence, gender-based abuse, intimate partner violence* (Dobash and Dobash 2015).

Theories in this field have been largely based on the findings of clinical and epidemiological studies of women and children who have been abused, as well as population studies on partner violence. The most groundbreaking theory of violence in intimate relationships since the 1990s is to be found in sociologist Michael P. Johnson's empirically based typologies of *intimate terrorism* and *situational violence* (Johnson 1995, 2008). Johnson defines intimate terrorism as a partner's use of serious physical and/or sexual violence combined with various control strategies that either directly or indirectly aim to dominate the partner. Such control strategies may include the use of emotional abuse, isolation, threats, humiliation, harassment and influencing the children to turn against the partner (Johnson and Leone 2005). Intimate terrorism and situational violence are concepts that are also used in today's research to identify and classify violent acts and patterns of violence, and have been central in the design of questionnaires in both international and Nordic prevalence studies of violence in intimate relationships. The three most recent Norwegian studies into violence have utilised Johnson's typologies in designing questionnaires to identify various patterns of violent behaviour in partner violence (Thoresen and Hjemdal 2014; Haaland et al. 2005; Pape and Stefansen 2004).

Johnson's typologies are also dominant in international research in the field. Advocates of both the gender symmetry perspective (Archer 2002; Straus 2011) and the more traditional feminist perspective on men's violence against women (Kimmel 2002; Dobash and Dobash 2004, 2015) take Johnson's concepts as a starting point for their discussions.

Implicit in Johnson's perspective on intimate terrorism is a theory of gender power based on the idea that men as a group dominate women as a group, and that serious systematic physical violence and control are motivated by a desire for dominance and oppression. The socially defined gender roles lead to victimisation of women. Johnson (2006, 2011) claims that it is generally men who perpetrate this form of partner violence and that the motivation is linked to men's need to dominate women.

Australian researchers Sarah Wendt and Lana Zannettino discuss this in their book *Domestic Violence in Miscellaneous Contexts*, pointing out that Johnson asserts that "almost all" those perpetrators who feel the need to control their partners are men:

> The indication "almost all" is used here to acknowledge that this type of violence has been identified in lesbian relationships and that some women terrorise their male partner but, as Johnson (2011) has argued and distinguished over time, the primary perpetrators in heterosexual couples are men, and gender plays an important role. (Wendt and Zannettino 2015, p. 3)

Wendt and Zannettino use Johnson to assert that there are grounds to focus on male perpetrators and female victims. And their book does in fact deal with female victims. Over the last ten years, however, there has been a growing recognition that men can also be subjected to serious and systematic violence, from both women and men. Norwegian and international prevalence studies have included different forms of control strategies based on Johnson's typologies, and used them in various ways to distinguish those individuals who are subjected to extensive control combined with severe physical and sexual violence (intimate terrorism) from other victims of violence.

Despite Johnson arguing in his later work that some women perpetrate violence that can be defined as intimate terrorism, he continues to claim that the vast majority of "intimate terrorists" are men: "intimate terrorism is perpetrated almost exclusively by men". Johnson has therefore focused on male perpetrators in his work.

> With respect to implications for the question of gender symmetry, these types of domestic violence differ dramatically. In heterosexual relationships, intimate terrorism is perpetrated almost exclusively by men, whereas violent resistance is found almost exclusively among women. The other two types are gender symmetric. (Johnson 2006, p. 1003)

Several researchers have attempted to criticise Johnson's typologies and his emphasis on men's violence against women, and have made increasing efforts to establish that there is far more symmetry between men and women in both situational violence and intimate terrorism than he claims (Morgan and Wells 2016; Dutton 2011; Straus 2011; Hines and Douglas 2010a, b). Straus, for example, works within another theoretical paradigm, claiming that the use of violence must be seen in the light of earlier experiences of violence through which perpetrators have learned to accept violence in childhood, either as victims or as witnesses to violence, and that this can explain the gender symmetry which is found in prevalence studies (Straus 2011). Other, more individualising theories, such as social learning theory, have influenced programmes for perpetrators of violence with the aim of teaching perpetrators new non-violent strategies for dealing with family conflict (see Scott 2004). Dutton (2012) argues from the perspective of personality and that the role of early attachments and past childhood experiences can make some people more prone to partner violence than others (see also Follingstad et al. 2002).

Another form of violence that Johnson identifies, which is the most common form in intimate relationships, is *situational couple violence*. This form of partner violence is not linked with a general pattern of (or desire for) general control and dominance; rather, these episodes of violence are a result of a situational conflict that may be triggered by everyday stress or discussion escalating into violence (Johnson and Leone 2005, p. 323). Such violence is termed milder and is believed to have less serious consequences for the individual than the violence defined as intimate terrorism. Relationships between those couples affected by this are assumed to be more equal, and both parties can exercise violence. Despite this episodic and situational violence being "mild" or less detrimental, this does not mean that it is altogether harmless, nor that it cannot lead to fatal consequences (Johnson and Leone 2005). If a relationship is dominated by conflict and such violence occurs frequently, this may cause one or both parties to suffer mental and physical injury (Johnson 2008, p. 63).

Central to Johnson's thinking is that situational partner violence and intimacy terrorism follow different patterns. In his later work, Johnson introduced the concepts of *mutual violent control* and *violent resistance* (Johnson and Ferraro 2000; Johnson 2008). Violent resistance denotes physical violence that is exercised when the victim of intimate terrorism uses physical violence in situations as a form of self-defence. This is violence exercised in specific situations such as a violent response or counter-reaction to a partner's ongoing violence, dominance and control (Johnson 2008). We find that neither mutual violence nor violent resistance is particularly relevant to our material. On the contrary, the men we have interviewed tell us that they are proud of not having reacted to violence with violence. In some situations, the men held the women back, grasped them or even laid them on the ground to avoid being exposed to violence themselves. In such instances, men use their physical superiority to defend themselves, but this could not be seen as violent resistance.

We wish to point out that we find Johnson's perspective too narrow, and that it hinders both research on female perpetrators and any general understanding and acceptance that male victims in heterosexual relationships exist. Our research is thus a contribution to the understanding of the intimate terrorism to which men are exposed.

References

Allen-Collinson, J. (2009a). A Marked Man: Female-Perpetrated Intimate Partner Abuse. *International Journal of Men's Health, 8*(1), 22–40.

Allen-Collinson, J. (2009b). Intimate Intrusions Revisited: A Case of Intimate Partner Abuse and Violations of the Territories of the Self. *Qualitative Sociology Review, 5*(1), 50–69.

Archer, J. (2002). Sex Differences in Physically Aggressive Acts Between Heterosexual Partners: A Meta-Analytic Review. *Aggression and Violent Behavior, 7*(4), 313–351.

Corbally, M. (2015). Accounting for Intimate Partner Violence. *Journal of Interpersonal Violence, 30*(17), 3112–3132.

Dobash, R. P., & Dobash, R. E. (2004). Women's Violence to Men in Intimate Relationships: Working on a Puzzle. *British Journal of Criminology, 44*(3), 324–349.

Dobash, R. E., & Dobash, R. P. (2015). Domestic Violence: Sociological Perspectives. In *International Encyclopedia of the Social & Behavioral Sciences* (2nd ed., pp. 632–635). Elsevier.

Dutton, D. (2011). The Case Against the Role of Gender in Intimate Partner Violence. *Aggression and Violent Behavior, 17*(1), 99–104.

Dutton, D. (2012). Attachment Insecurity and Intimate Partner Violence. *Aggression and Violent Behavior, 17*(5), 475–481.

Follingstad, D., Bradley, R., Helff, C., & Laughlin, J. (2002). A Model for Predicting Dating Violence: Anxious Attachment, Angry Temperament, and Need for Relationship Control. *Violence and Victims, 17*(1), 35–47.

Haaland, T., Clausen, S., & Schei, B. (2005). *Vold i parforhold—ulike perspektiver: Resultater fra den første landsdekkende undersøkelsen i Norge (Violence in Partner Relationships—Various Perspectives: Results from the First Nationwide Survey in Norway)* (Vol. 2005:3, NIBR-rapport). Oslo: Norsk institutt for by- og regionforskning (Norwegian Institute for Urban and Regional Research). Retrieved from http://www.hioa.no/Om-HiOA/Senter-for-velferds-og-arbeidslivsforskning/NIBR/Publikasjoner/Publikasjoner-norsk/Vold-i-parforhold-ulike-perspektiver.

Hines, D., & Douglas, E. (2010a). A Closer Look at Men Who Sustain Intimate Terrorism by Women. *Partner Abuse, 1*(3), 286–313.

Hines, D., & Douglas, E. (2010b). Intimate Terrorism by Women Towards Men: Does It Exist? *Journal of Aggression, Conflict and Peace Research, 2*(3), 36–56.

Isdal, P. (2000). *Meningen med volden. (The Meaning with the Violence)* Oslo: Kommuneforlaget.

Johnson, M. P. (1995). Patriarchal Terrorism and Common Couple Violence: Two Forms of Violence Against Women. *Journal of Marriage and Family, 57*(2), 283–294.

Johnson, M. (2006). Conflict and Control. *Violence Against Women, 12*(11), 1003–1018.

Johnson, M. (2008). *A Typology of Domestic Violence: Intimate Terrorism, Violent Resistance, and Situational Couple Violence.* Boston: Northeastern University Press.

Johnson, M. (2011). Gender and Types of Intimate Partner Violence: A Response to an Anti-feminist Literature Review. *Aggression and Violent Behavior, 16*(4), 289–296.

Johnson, M. P., & Ferraro, K. (2000). Research on Domestic Violence in the 1990s: Making Distinctions. *Journal of Marriage and Family, 62*(4), 948–963.

Johnson, M. P., & Leone, J. M. (2005). The Differential Effects of Intimate Terrorism and Situational Couple Violence: Findings from the National Violence Against Women Survey. *Journal of Family Issues, 26*(3), 322–349.

Kimmel, M. (2002). "Gender Symmetry" in Domestic Violence. *Violence Against Women, 8*(11), 1332–1363.

Krug, E. (2002). *World Report on Violence and Health.* Geneva: World Health Organization. Retrieved from http://www.who.int/violence_injury_prevention/violence/world_report/en/.

Morgan, W., & Wells, M. (2016). It's Deemed Unmanly': Men's Experiences of Intimate Partner Violence (IPV). *The Journal of Forensic Psychiatry & Psychology, 27*(3), 1–15.

Pape, H., & Stefansen, K. (2004). *Den Skjulte volden?: En undersøkelse av Oslobefolkningens utsatthet for trusler, vold og seksuelle overgrep (The Hidden Violence?: A Study of the Vulnerability to Threats, Violence and Sexual Assault of Oslo's Population)* (Vol. Nr 1/2004, Rapport (Nasjonalt kunnskapssenter om vold og traumatisk stress: online)). Nasjonalt kunnskapssenter om vold og traumatisk stress (The Norwegian Centre for Violence and Traumatic Stress Studies). Retrieved from https://www.nkvts.no/rapport/den-skjulte-volden-en-undersokelse-av-oslobefolkningens-utsatthet-for-trusler-vold-og-seksuelle-overgrep/.

Richardson, D. (2005). The Myth of Female Passivity: Thirty Years of Revelations About Female Aggression. *Psychology of Women Quarterly, 29*(3), 238–247.

Scott, K. (2004). Predictors of Change Among Male Batterers: Application of Theories and Review of Empirical Findings. *Trauma, Violence & Abuse, 5*(3), 260–284.

Sogn, H., & Hjemdal, O. K. (2009). *Vold mot menn i nære relasjoner: Kunnskapsgjennomgang og rapport fra et pilotprosjekt (Violence Against Men in Intimate Relationships: A Review of Current Knowledge and Report from a Pilot Project).* Oslo: Norsk kunnskapssenter om vold og traumatisk stress (The Norwegian Centre for Violence and Traumatic Stress Studies) (NKVTS). Retrieved from https://www.nkvts.no/rapport/vold-mot-menn-i-naere-relasjoner/.

Straus, M. (2011). Gender Symmetry and Mutuality in Perpetration of Clinical-Level Partner Violence: Empirical Evidence and Implications for Prevention and Treatment. *Aggression and Violent Behavior, 16*(4), 279–288.

Thoresen, S., & Hjemdal, O. K. (2014). *Vold og voldtekt i Norge: En nasjonal forekomststudie av vold i et livsløpsperspektiv (Violence and Rape in Norway: A national prevalence study of violence in a lifespan perspective)* (Vol. 1/2014, Report (Nasjonalt kunnskapssenter om vold og traumatisk stress: published version) (The Norwegian Centre for Violence and Traumatic Stress Studies)). Oslo: Nasjonalt kunnskapssenter om vold og traumatisk stress (The Norwegian Centre for Violence and Traumatic Stress Studies). Retrieved from https://www.nkvts.no/rapport/vold-og-voldtekt-i-norge-en-nasjonal-forekomststudie-av-vold-i-et-livslopsperspektiv/.

Wendt, S., & Zannettino, L. (2015). *Domestic Violence in Diverse Context: A Re-examination of Gender.* London and New York: Routledge.

Open Access This chapter is licensed under the terms of the Creative Commons Attribution 4.0 International License (http://creativecommons.org/licenses/by/4.0/), which permits use, sharing, adaptation, distribution and reproduction in any medium or format, as long as you give appropriate credit to the original author(s) and the source, provide a link to the Creative Commons licence and indicate if changes were made.

The images or other third party material in this chapter are included in the chapter's Creative Commons licence, unless indicated otherwise in a credit line to the material. If material is not included in the chapter's Creative Commons licence and your intended use is not permitted by statutory regulation or exceeds the permitted use, you will need to obtain permission directly from the copyright holder.

2

Method and Analysis

Review of Nordic Studies

Our aim here was to collect data, information and conclusions provided by previous surveys for reference and comparison. We have reviewed key Nordic prevalence studies that chart the extent of violence against men in intimate relationships.

The research literature on partner violence is considerably more extensive than the research on violence against men in other intimate relationships, and throughout we reflect on our lack of knowledge about violence against men within friendships, the family and other relationships of trust. The majority of Nordic prevalence studies of violence in intimate relationships focus on violence in heterosexual relationships, and the Nordic literature on violence in gay relationships is very limited. We found only one prevalence study in this field. We also found no Nordic prevalence studies on honour-related violence/forced marriage in our review of the available literature. The Norwegian health surveys contained very few questions about violence. In two major Norwegian studies, Helseundersøkelsen i Oslo (Health Survey in Oslo; HUBRO) and Helseundersøkelsen i Hordland (Health Survey in Hordaland; HUSK), only women were asked questions about violence.

© The Author(s) 2019   **13**
M. I. Lien, J. Lorentzen, *Men's Experiences of Violence in Intimate Relationships*,
Palgrave Studies in Victims and Victimology,
https://doi.org/10.1007/978-3-030-03994-3_2

Our main aim has been to look at studies dealing with violence towards adult men (over 18 years old). We have not, in our review of the literature, been able to throw light on the risk factors or variations in vulnerability between different groups of men. We have, to a limited degree, found statistics relating to the prevalence of violence against men from the wider family, friends and acquaintances/colleagues. The majority of studies that highlight violence from the wider family and friends are oriented towards men under the age of 18.

Survey

We conducted an internet survey to investigate the level of awareness among the Norwegian public of the available support services, including crisis centres, family protection offices and centres against incest and sexual abuse, and the level of public awareness that these can (also) be accessed by men.

Qualitative Study of Male Victims of Violence

The aim of this qualitative study was to gain greater insight into men's experiences of violence, and to contribute new and relevant knowledge to a research field that has been dominated by research into women's experiences of violence. There is little knowledge about, or understanding of, men's experience of violence in intimate relationships, so that these interviews with vulnerable men represent part of a project to improve visibility. The purpose of this study is to throw light on how men live with violence and how they deal with their experiences.

The questions we address in this qualitative part of the study concern the kinds of experiences men have in intimate relationships, the relationships in which violence occurs and the consequences this violence has for men. Furthermore, we have asked men about their experiences of the available support services and how the help on offer might be improved.

The interview study consists of in-depth interviews with 28 men who have been subjected to various forms of violence in intimate relationships. The vast majority (26 men) are current or former users of family protection services, crisis centres or centres against incest and sexual assault. In addition to posing questions about their experience of violence, the interviews also include questions about their early childhood experiences, their backgrounds and upbringing, and family relationships. We have asked about the psychological, emotional and social consequences of the violence on the daily lives of these men, and asked them to reflect on how they function in the workplace, within the family and in other areas of their lives.

The interviews were conducted from March to August 2016 by Claes Ekenstam, Jørgen Lorentzen and Marianne Inéz Lien. The interviews lasted for 1.5–2.5 hours and were transcribed verbatim.

Interviewees from Family Protection and Crisis Centres

At the very start of the project, we contacted three *family protection offices* which we knew had worked specifically with violence against men in close relationships. Initially we arranged for two of these offices to contact men whom they thought could contribute to our study. It was soon proved, however, that the selected offices had some difficulty in recruiting men, and with time being of the essence we sought potential interviewees through alternative channels. Four men were recruited through the snowball sampling method—that is, through colleagues who knew of men who had been exposed to violence in intimate relationships, and who asked these men if they wanted to participate in our interviews. Furthermore, we recruited six men by posting information about the project on Facebook and Proba's website. One of the men we wanted to interview withdrew immediately before the interview, so that our final number of interviewees was nine. All nine are heterosexual, ethnic Norwegian men between the ages of 28 and 66. Seven of them have children. They have all experienced violence from a present or former female partner. Eight out of the nine men have used the services of various family protection offices around the country.

We have also interviewed nine men who have used various *crisis centres* in Norway. We deliberately sought to recruit a wide range of men in this sample, with special emphasis on including men of immigrant background.

Six out of the nine men in this sample come from foreign backgrounds. There were two reasons for our desire to include this group of men. Firstly, our knowledge of violence against men from immigrant backgrounds is almost non-existent; secondly, statistics from Norwegian crisis centres show that the percentage of immigrant users is high and that their numbers have increased in recent years. Three of the nine men have experienced violence from gay partners. In this area too, previous knowledge is inadequate.

In the book, we refer to the interviewees as either foreign or Norwegian, and give no further details of their origins so as to protect their identity. These interviewees have been given names that offer the reader some sense of regional background. Several of our contributors have partners from foreign backgrounds. We mention partners as either foreign or Norwegian.

Interviewees from the Centre Against Incest and Sexual Abuse

We conducted ten interviews with men who have been subjected to sexual abuse as children or adolescents, and in some cases as adults. All these men have, as a result of this abuse, sought help at one of Norway's centres against incest and sexual abuse. The interviews were conducted at, and in collaboration with, two of these centres in spring 2016.

All the interviewees were ethnic Norwegian. Most were between 36 and 48 years old, one was younger (28 years old) and two were over 60 years old. This sample represents a wide range of men with various occupations and in differing circumstances. Some lived alone with or without their children, or were divorced. Others were married or were living with partners, with or without their children or stepchildren, or had children (and grandchildren) who were living elsewhere.

In planning the interviews, we also wanted to ask about the experiences of the professionals who meet these men. Early on in the project, we held discussions with staff from all three of the above support agencies to get an insight into the issues that might be important to highlight in our interviews.

Interview Methods

The interviews were designed with the intention of getting descriptions of everyday events and encouraging men to reflect on their lived experiences (Ellis and Flaherty 1992). We chose an open and inquiring approach where the men were allowed to tell their stories in their own time; we were keen that they should put their experiences in their own words and have time to reflect on possible links between their childhood experiences and adult experiences of violence. The interviews were set up as semi-structured life-story interviews (Atkinson 1998).

This interview technique is inspired by phenomenology. In the context of qualitative studies, the phenomenological approach aims to get insight into a particular phenomenon from the perspective of the actors, describing the world as perceived by them and exploring meaning through their experiences. This interpretive phenomenological analysis (IPA) is concerned with the personal perception of the informants' experiences (Smith et al. 1999). This is particularly important in research that affects people's physical and mental health and rehabilitation (Kvale and Brinkmann 2009). We used the same opening questions with each interviewee, with which we focused on topics relevant to the study, without being locked into a standardised template. Connections and patterns in the experiences of subjects, as well as varying perceptions and different aspects of the phenomena themselves, can then be captured.

Ethical Considerations

Violence is a sensitive issue, and we have been delicate and attentive in our approach to gain access to the men's experiences. We were particularly concerned that the men should be able to control how much they said about actual incidents of violence. Each interviewee was given a letter explaining what their information would be used for.

The interviews of men from the centres against incest and sexual abuse were conducted at the centres by a researcher in our team who is a qualified psychotherapist with long experience in talking to men who are victims of violence. Sexual abuse can, in particular, be very difficult to talk about. We established good relationships with members of staff at all the centres, in particular with those staff at the centre against incest and sexual abuse who recruited interviewees. To ensure proper ongoing support throughout and after the project, it was agreed that staff would be on the premises during the interviews and would offer the men a debriefing afterwards if and when it was needed.

In order to ensure a sense of security around the informants from the crisis centres, the interviews were conducted in the centres' premises during the day. Staff were available to talk to afterwards. Interviews with the men from family protection were generally conducted on the premises of Proba Social Analysis, and all the interviewees were encouraged to make contact if they needed to talk afterwards.

All the interviews were transcribed in their entirety. Names, places and other information that might be a risk to anonymity were omitted during the transcription process. We have used fictional names for the interviewees throughout. We have omitted any details about occupation and education to further ensure anonymity. The project has been approved by the Personvernombudet (NSD; Norwegian Data Protection Agency for Research).

Analysis and Preparation

These interviews form part of a project aimed at increasing the visibility of male victims of violence. We have, in the presentation of our empirical data, put emphasis on giving detailed descriptions of men's experiences of violence and abuse, and their understanding of the situations in which it occurs and its consequences in their lives.

Those men recruited through crisis centres and family protection offices have all been the subject of partner violence and thus share similar experiences of violence, but have very different profiles. The men with experience of crisis centres are current users of their centre and have been exposed to violence recently. Their backgrounds are various. The sample includes both ethnic Norwegians and men from immigrant backgrounds. Three of the men have experience of partner violence in gay relationships.

The variety of backgrounds from which the men come adds breadth to the narrative about men's experience of violence in intimate relationships.

The majority of men who have had contact with family protection have experiences of violence that date from more than five years ago. This allows the study to provide insight into the long-term effects of partner violence. This sample also consists of men who have attended family protection offices for mediation. Their experiences of violence have often been left unmentioned during this mediation. This is reflected in Chap. 5.

The interviewees recruited through incest centres have suffered abuse in childhood and adolescence, and describe the profound psychological and social consequences that this violence has had on them. In our analysis of these men, therefore, there is a greater focus on the kinds of trauma that have been caused by this violence than there is in the analysis of the other men's experiences in Chap. 4.

References

Atkinson, R. (1998). *The Life Story Interview*. Thousand Oaks, CA: Sage.

Ellis, C., & Flaherty, M. (1992). *Investigating Subjectivity: Research on Lived Experience* (Vol. 139, Sage focus editions). Newbury Park, CA: Sage.

Kvale, S., & Brinkmann, S. (2009). *Interviews: Learning the Craft of Qualitative Research Interviewing* (2nd ed.). Los Angeles, CA: Sage.

Smith, J., Jarman, M., & Osborn, M. (1999). Doing Interpretative Phenomenological Analysis. In M. Murray & K. Chamberlain (Eds.), *Qualitative Health Psychology: Theories and Methods* (pp. 218–240). London: SAGE Publications Ltd.

Open Access This chapter is licensed under the terms of the Creative Commons Attribution 4.0 International License (http://creativecommons.org/licenses/by/4.0/), which permits use, sharing, adaptation, distribution and reproduction in any medium or format, as long as you give appropriate credit to the original author(s) and the source, provide a link to the Creative Commons licence and indicate if changes were made.

The images or other third party material in this chapter are included in the chapter's Creative Commons licence, unless indicated otherwise in a credit line to the material. If material is not included in the chapter's Creative Commons licence and your intended use is not permitted by statutory regulation or exceeds the permitted use, you will need to obtain permission directly from the copyright holder.

3

Prevalence Studies from the Nordic Countries

Nordic prevalence studies show that both women and men are exposed to partner violence. However, the statistics vary greatly from one report to another. It is reasonable to assume that this is largely as a result of variations in the definitions that each uses of violence, differences in method and/or bias in samples or, indeed, coincidence. Although in some studies the percentage is low, there are nonetheless many men who have been exposed to violence. A finding that appears regularly is that more women than men are exposed to serious physical partner violence, but in the case of less serious physical violence, gender differences are considerably smaller. In some studies, the proportion of women and men exposed to less serious physical violence is almost equal. Psychological violence is the form of violence to which both women and men are most often subject. However, the statistics vary hugely according to the way the concept of psychological violence is operationalised in the investigations. This is primarily dependent upon the precise range of control strategies included in each study. Both men and women are exposed to various forms of controlling behaviour by partners.

© The Author(s) 2019   **21**
M. I. Lien, J. Lorentzen, *Men's Experiences of Violence in Intimate Relationships*,
Palgrave Studies in Victims and Victimology,
https://doi.org/10.1007/978-3-030-03994-3_3

Several of the prevalence studies are designed to capture violence within certain time frames, although these time frames may vary (one year ago, the last five years, earlier in life and/or throughout life). There may also be differences in the diversity of samples, and to what extent all sections of the population are included. It is reasonable to assume that marginalised groups, such as addicts, criminals, the mentally ill and homeless people, may be substantially under-represented in nationwide prevalence studies and other surveys. We know from clinical studies that these groups are particularly vulnerable to violence. Additionally, it is rare in prevalence studies to ask the respondent if they are *both* a victim and a perpetrator of violence in intimate relationships, although some studies include victims' own violence and can therefore, to some extent, distinguish mutual violence.

The methodological challenges mean it is difficult to make any direct comparison of the findings from these prevalence studies.

Consequences of Violence Towards Men in Intimate Relationships

Most studies investigate the consequences of violence in general. Few of the prevalence studies we have looked at deal with the consequences of partner violence and the help that men seek.

In the prevalence study *Vold og voldtekt i Norge* (*Violence and Rape in Norway*; Thoresen and Hjemdal 2014), it was found that men who are exposed to physical violence in general (not exclusively in intimate relationships) often suffer from physical damage in the form of scarring and bruising, internal injuries or fractures. In this study, 53.1 per cent of men and 55.7 per cent of women who answered that they had been exposed to serious violence reported that they had suffered injuries (p. 77); 31.6 per cent of men and 49.6 per cent of women answered that they had been afraid that they might be seriously injured or killed when the violence was taking place. Most of the men were exposed to violence from unknown persons (72.1 per cent). The majority of women were exposed to serious violence by partners (40.9 per cent). The study found an increased risk of mental health problems in both men and women who had been subjected to violence and rape compared to those who had not (p. 98).

In the *Stockholms-undersøkelsen* (Stockholm survey; Bååk 2013), 15 per cent of men and 39 per cent of women who had been exposed to serious violence reported that one or more of the incidents of violence in the previous year had resulted in injuries that led to, or should have led to, their visiting a doctor, nurse or dentist (p. 34). In *Brottförebyggande rådets undersøkelse fra 2012* (Swedish National Council for Crime Prevention study 2012; Frenzel 2014), 2.4 per cent of men and 29.1 per cent of women who were exposed to serious violence reported that they visited or should have visited a doctor, nurse or dentist (p. 49).

In the study *Vold i parforhold—ulike perspektiver* (*Violence in Partner Relationships—Various Perspectives*), Haaland and his fellow researchers found that many of those exposed to violence reported that they had been unable to protect themselves from that violence, and 2.2 per cent of the men and 8.4 per cent of the women stated that they were exposed to violence with a "very high potential for injury" (Haaland et al. 2005, p. 60). One in ten men reported serious physical injuries as a direct consequence of the partner violence which they had experienced (p. 108).

The Swedish study "Self-Reported Exposure to Intimate Partner Violence Among Women and Men in Sweden: Results from a Population-Based Survey" (Nybergh et al. 2013) measured the social consequences of partner violence. The study found that men reported varying social consequences of partner violence, but here N is very small: 26 men and 58 women. A larger proportion of women than men left the family home and divorced as a result of the violence. A larger proportion of men worked longer hours to get away from home.

In the 2005 *Danske kjærestevoldundersøkelsen* (*Danish Violence between Couples Survey*), almost half of the young men who had suffered physical violence from a partner reported that this violence had not affected them. However, one in three young men stated that they had experienced feelings of guilt at being the victim of partner violence, and 22 per cent of men had felt hatred or hopelessness as a result of violence (Schütt et al. 2008, p. 66). Additionally, a significant correlation between sexual assault and suicide attempts was demonstrated in men, although the data material was thin.

In the 2005 Danish health survey *SUSY*, it was found that men who have experienced violence report low moods and suicide attempts more often than those who have not, but also that male victims report better health than female victims (Helweg-Larsen and Frederiksen 2008, p. 6).

In the Swedish study "Men's and Women's Exposure and Perpetration of Partner Violence" (Lövestad and Krantz 2012), men who were exposed to mental partner violence reported having suicidal thoughts. No men exposed to physical partner violence reported the same.

In the 2009 *Finske studien om vold mot menn i nære relasjoner* (*Finnish Study of Violence against Men in Close Relationships;* Heiskanen and Ruuskanen 2011), 9.7 per cent of men and 35.2 per cent of women reported that they had suffered psychological problems as a result of partner violence from their current partner (N = 203 men and 138 women); 21 per cent of men and 60.6 per cent of women reported that they had suffered psychological problems as a result of partner violence from former partners (N = 221 men and 300 women; p. 22). The psychological problems most frequently experienced by women included fear, hatred and low self-esteem/feelings of vulnerability. Those most usual among men included depression, shock and hatred.

Consistent in many studies is the fact that women report greater psychological problems as a result of partner violence. However, Norwegian interview studies with men at crisis centres (Grøvdal and Jonassen 2015; Danielsen 2013) find that men who experience serious and systematic partner violence have many of the same psychological responses as women: social isolation, anxiety and fear of further violence. Another consistent finding in interview studies of women exposed to serious partner violence is that many find psychological violence the most difficult to recover from (Grøvdal and Jonassen 2015; Danielsen 2013; Bjerkeseth 2010; Storberget et al. 2007).

What Help Do Male Victims of Violence Seek?

The prevalence studies we have reviewed all, to a limited degree, investigate the help sought by men who experience violence. To the extent that these studies deal with this subject, the focus is purely on the care available after physical violence. The studies indicate that many male victims of violence conceal incidents of violence from others and do not contact any support services or report the violence to the police.

In the prevalence study of violence and rape in Norway (Thoresen and Hjemdal 2014), fully 59.1 per cent of the men who had experienced minor violence from a partner reported that they had never spoken to anyone about this violence. Less than a fifth of the men had talked to health professionals about their experiences of serious physical violence (p. 124). Most of the women who had experienced minor violence had talked to others about the violence; only 21.9 per cent of the women had never spoken to others about the violence (p. 79).

In the same study, 24 men reported that they had been raped. None said that they had undergone any medical examination or treatment in the days or weeks following the rape (p. 88). Out of the 24 men, 4 (16.7 per cent) had reported the rape.

In the study *Vold i parforhold—ulike perspektiver* (*Violence in Partner Relationships—Alternative Perspectives*), Haaland et al. (2005) found that only one in ten men who were exposed to partner violence, who had stayed in the relationship, had talked to someone about the violence. Of those who had split up from their partners, little more than 10 per cent had sought help from one or more support agencies (p. 151). In comparison, nearly a third of women who had split up with their partners had sought help from support agencies.

The Oslo survey (Pape and Stefansen 2004) showed that only one in four men and one in three women subjected to partner violence had contacted the police, or other professionals or support agencies. These findings are confirmed by the *Violence and Rape Study* from 2014.

In the survey *Våldsamt lika och ulika—Om vold i samkönade parrelationer* (*Violence Equal and Unequal—Violence in Cohabiting Couples*; Holmberg et al. 2005), it was found that only 6 per cent of men who had experienced violence had reported it to the police.

In the 2009 Finnish study of violence against men in intimate relationships (Heiskanen and Ruuskanen 2011), only 0.5 per cent of the men who had suffered violence from their current partner reported that they had contacted the police, and 1.9 per cent of the men who were victims of violence from a former partner reported that they had been in contact with the police (p. 36).

In Denmark, of the 14,753 cases of violence against men reported to the police in the period 2008–2009, only 1 per cent were defined as partner violence. This corresponds to a figure of 2 men per 100,000 men aged 16–79 who reported partner violence to the police (Plauborg and Helweg-Larsen 2012, p. 10). Between 2008 and 2010, each Danish police district received an average of 1–2 inquiries from men exposed to sexual violence (p. 70). The Danish Accident Register shows that about 300 men per year contact emergency services due to partner violence (p. 11). If we see this in the light of the 2010 Danish SUSY survey, which estimates that 8000 men are the subject of physical partner violence annually, this implies that very few men report the violence or seek emergency medical assistance.

Table 3.1 summarises the main findings in the surveys on the numbers of men exposed to partner violence. In the case of both physical and psychological violence, there are major differences between countries, and occasionally between the various studies within each country.

Both women and men are exposed to partner violence. However, the results showing its prevalence in the various studies can vary enormously. It is reasonable to assume that this is largely a consequence of differences in the definition of violence, variations in method and/or coincidences/bias in sample groups. In the case of physical violence, the studies from Denmark show a much lower proportion than other countries. With the exception of one Swedish study with a very high proportion of physical violence once in the last year, the figures for Norway and Sweden are at approximately the same level. There is only one Finnish study, and it shows that a high proportion of people have experienced violence. In the case of psychological violence, there is only one Danish study, and in this area that study again shows the lowest proportion of victims of violence. With the exception of one Swedish study whose figures are high, there is again a reasonable correlation between studies from Norway and Sweden. Once more, the Finnish study shows a higher incidence than those from elsewhere.

All the studies demonstrate that partner violence also affects men. Although the percentage shown in some of the studies is low, there are nonetheless many men who have been exposed to violence. Psychological violence is a form of violence that particularly affects men. It is therefore important that studies that identify the presence of violence against men in intimate relationships include psychological violence.

Table 3.1 Numbers of men exposed to partner violence

Name of study	Year	Country	Minor physical violence				Serious physical violence				Psychological violence				Sexual violence			
			Last year		Once in lifetime		Last year		Once in lifetime		Last year		Once in lifetime		Last year		Once in lifetime	
			M	F	M	F	M	F	M	F	M	F	M	F	M	F	M	F
Thoresen & Hjemdal	2014	Norway			16.3	14.4			1.9	9.2							0.1	3.8
Haaland et al.	2005	Norway	5.6	5.7	21.8	27.1			2.6	9.2			3	5.1				
Pape & Stefansen	2004	Norway	11	9			3	2	3	12	2	6	7	15				
Andersson et al.	2014	Sweden	1.2		5	14					2.5	4.8	8	20			1	7
Frenzel	2014	Sweden	2	2.2	8.1	15					6.2	6.8	14.5	23.5			0.3	3.6
Nyberg et al.	2013	Sweden	7.6	8.1	6.8	14.3					24	24	14	24	2.3	3	2.5	9
Bååk	2013	Sweden	3	2.6	13	22							23	37			2	11
Lovenstad & Krantz	2012	Sweden	11	8	11	15.9					24	23.6	37	41	0.6	3.2	3.5	9.6
SUSY study	2010	Denmark	0.5															
Survey of Violence in Love Relationships	2011	Denmark	1.7	3.2							1.5				1.2	2.7		
Heiskanen & Ruuskanen	2011	Finland	4.4–14.2	3.7–14.3	19.5	36.5							36.4		0.7	2.3	1.6	12.6

The statistical findings of these surveys differ greatly, but nonetheless certain trends emerge. More women than men experience serious physical partner violence. Women also report more significant psychological difficulties as a result of partner violence in general. In the case of less serious physical violence, the disparity between genders is considerably smaller; in some studies the percentage of women and men exposed to less severe physical violence is almost equal. Men are rarely exposed to sexual partner violence. Psychological violence is the form of violence to which the majority of both women and men are exposed. The gender difference in the proportion of women to men who are exposed to psychological violence also varies greatly between studies. Some studies show that the proportion of men exposed to psychological violence is almost as high as the proportion of women; others show a significantly higher incidence among women than among men. Psychological violence is defined very differently in the studies, depending primarily on the extent to which different forms of control strategies are included. We see that both women and men experience controlling behaviour from partners. Several of the surveys also show that the majority of those subjected to serious partner violence are also subjected to controlling behaviour.

Violence research finds that both men and women are exposed more often to psychological violence than physical violence, and that this applies even more to men than to women. Both Nordic and international research has shown that both men and women feel that psychological violence has major consequences for their mental health and quality of life. In order to capture the types of violence to which men are most often exposed, it is essential to have a deeper understanding of the ways in which psychological violence operates.

Norwegian Survey

The last part of this chapter deals with that part of the study which investigates the level of awareness in Norway of the support available through crisis centres, family protection services and centres against incest and sexual abuse, and the awareness that these bodies also offer help to men. We conducted a survey to find out the level of awareness about these services (1) in the general population; (2) among staff of support agencies; and (3) among those who have been victims of violence in intimate relationships.

Our survey shows that crisis centres are the service best known about, with 81 per cent of respondents saying they are aware of what these centres offer; 56 per cent record that they are aware of the family protection office and 50 per cent that they know about the centres against incest and sexual abuse. The family protection office is a low-threshold service offered to families experiencing problems, and offers mandatory mediation in the case of separation and relationship breakdown between parents with children under the age of 16. Despite the fact that this is a service with a broad target group, the family protection office is a little-known organisation. Crisis centres and the centres against incest and sexual abuse by contrast have a far more limited target group, but are as well known as the family protection office.

A positive finding is that respondents who, based on their field of work/employment, can be described as health workers show a greater awareness of all three services than the general public. These services are also better known among men who have been victims of violence than among respondents in general (Fig. 3.1).

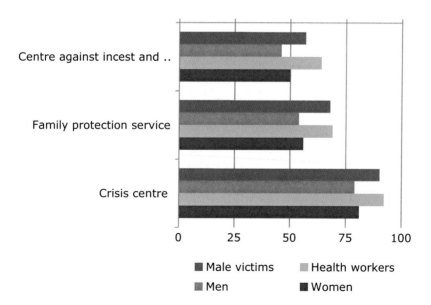

Fig. 3.1 Percentage of those aware of the services available to victims of violence in intimate relationships

What is interesting is that the proportion is halved when we ask if respondents know that the crisis centres also offer their services to men who are subjected to violence. Only 41 per cent of respondents know that crisis centres offer help to men exposed to violence in intimate relationships. This is considerably fewer than those who know about crisis centres in general. Of those aware of the family protection office and centres against incest and sexual abuse, the proportions are 32 per cent and 27 per cent, respectively. Men who have been the victims of violence in intimate relationships differ to a small extent from other respondents in their response to this question.

Those we define as health workers show a greater awareness that these services are available to men. However, even among this group only around 50 per cent know that male victims of violence can use the services of crisis centres, and this figure drops to 40 per cent in the case of family protection offices and centres against incest and sexual abuse. These figures are somewhat surprising and indicate that awareness of the needs of men is very low, not only in the general population, but among those who are employed to offer such help.

Figure 3.2 shows the response distribution among the various groups of respondents.

Of the respondents who have been exposed to violence in intimate relationships, 35 per cent state that they could have benefited from or that they needed assistance in relation to these events; 46 per cent say they have not needed help, and 19 per cent do not know.

We asked those men who had been exposed to violence if they had been in contact with any organisations offering help as a result of these incidents. Only 2 per cent responded that they had been in contact with a crisis centre, 2 per cent that they had been in contact with family protection and 4 per cent that they had been in contact with a centre against incest and sexual abuse.

Moreover, 21 per cent responded that they had been in contact with other services. We asked an open question about which services they had been in contact with. Several men reported that they had been in contact with a doctor, others with the police.

We asked those men who had not sought help (N = 43) about their reasons for not doing so. Respondents could tick multiple response options. The most common reason selected is that the victim "wanted to

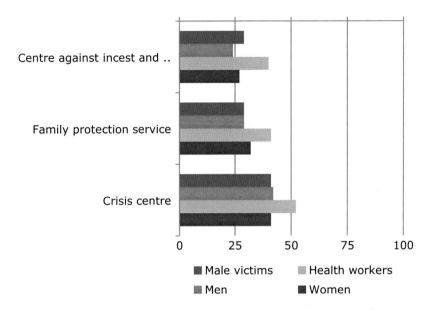

Fig. 3.2 Percentage of those aware of the services available to men subjected to violence in intimate relationships

handle it" on their own. Among those who have not sought help, over 60 per cent give this as their reason. A larger proportion of those who have been subjected to physical violence express that they would rather deal with it on their own (62 per cent) than those subjected to psychological violence (48 per cent). Many men responded that they do not generally seek help when they have problems and/or that they experience it as shameful to do so. Other respondents indicated that they feared the potential reaction of their partner or further abuse.

Just over 20 per cent responded that they did not know that the support agencies (crisis centres, family protection office and centres against incest and sexual abuse) offer their services to men.

Of the 700 men who responded to our survey, 9 per cent stated that they have been victims of violence from people with whom they have an intimate relationship, after the age of 18.

In the questionnaire we asked about the following forms of violence:

- Physical violence: kicking, hitting, pulling hair, biting, the use of weapons or other objects, or other forms of physical violence.

- Psychological violence: harassment, threats (including threats of not having contact with their children), controlling behaviour or other forms of psychological violence.
- Sexual violence: sexual harassment, rape, abuse or other sexual violence.

Of the respondents, 6.6 per cent indicated that they have been subjected to physical violence, 5.4 per cent that they have been subjected to psychological violence and 1.4 per cent that they have been subjected to sexual violence.

Of those who have been subjected to physical violence, 35 per cent reported that they have experienced such violence on 2–4 occasions, and 20 per cent that they have experienced it five times or more. Among those who have been subjected to psychological violence, 45 per cent said that they have experienced this form of violence five times or more.

Among those who have been victims of violence ($N = 60$), over half have been subjected to both physical and psychological violence. Just over 15 per cent have been experienced incidents of a physical and sexual nature, while around 15 per cent have been subjected to both psychological and sexual violence.

Of the 57 men who responded to the question about the gender of the perpetrator, 51 per cent reported that women perpetrated the violence and 39 per cent that men perpetrated the violence.

We asked the victims of violence what relationship they have/had to the person who perpetrated the violence: 54 per cent answered that it was a wife/partner/girlfriend, 26 per cent that it was a member of their close family, 7 per cent that it was someone from the wider family, while 11 per cent answered that it was someone else to whom they were close. The respondents could answer several categories.

References

Andersson, T., Heimer, G., & Lucas, S. (2014). *Forekomststudien Våld och hälsa—En befolkningsundersökning om kvinnors och mäns våldsutsatthet samt kopplingen til hälsa (A Prevalence Study of Violence and Health—A Population*

Survey on the Vulnerability of Women and Men and Links to Health). Nationellt centrum för kvinnofrid (National Centre for Women's Peace), NCK. Sweden: Uppsala University. Retrieved from http://nck.uu.se/kunskapsbanken/ amnesguider/att-mata-vald/befolkningsundersokningen-vald-och-halsa/.

Bååk, L. (2013) Karlägging av våld i nära relationer i Stockholms stad (Charting the Perpetration of Violence in the City of Stockholm). Social Administration: City of Stockholm. Retrieved from http://www5.goteborg.se/prod/ Intraservice/Namndhandlingar/SamrumPortal.nsf/93ec9160f537fa30c1257 2aa004b6c1a/131f5d1f612979cac125813f004c151c/$FILE/18B_Bilaga_ Kartlaggning_forekomst_vald_i_nara_relationer.pdf.

Bjerkeseth, L. B. (2010). *Den Mannlige Offerrollen: En Intervjustudie Av Menn Som Opplever Vold Fra Kvinnelig Partner (The Male Victim: An Interview Study of Men Who Experience Violence by Female Partners).* Master's dissertation, Institutt for sosiologi og samfunnsgeografi (Department of Sociology and Social Geography), University of Oslo. Retrieved from https://www.duo.uio. no/handle/10852/15305.

Danielsen, E. M. (2013). *"Jeg Følte Jeg Var En Slags Merkelig Fugl Som Hadde Flydd Inn Her": En Kvalitativ Intervjustudie Av Menns Møte Med Krisesentre ("I Felt Like a Strange Kind of Bird Who Had Flown in Here": A Qualitative Interview Study of Men's Encounter with Crisis Centres).* Master's dissertation, Department of Sociology and Social Geography, University of Oslo. Retrieved from https://www.duo.uio.no/handle/10852/36850.

Frenzel, A. (2014). *Brott i nära relationer. En nationell kartläggning (Crime in Intimate Relationships. A National Survey).* Stockholm: Crime Prevention Council. Retrieved from https://www.bra.se/download/18.9eaaede145606cc 8651ff/1399015861526/2014_8_Brott_i_nara_relationer.pdf.

Grøvdal, Y., Jonassen, W., & Nasjonalt kunnskapssenter om vold og traumatisk stress (The Norwegian Centre for Violence and Traumatic Stress Studies). (2015). *Menn på krisesenter* (Vol. 5/2015, Rapport (Nasjonalt kunnskaps-senter om vold og traumatisk stress: trykt utg)). Oslo: Nasjonalt kunnskaps-senter om vold og traumatisk stress (The Norwegian Centre for Violence and Traumatic Stress Studies). Retrieved from https://www.nkvts.no/rapport/ menn-pa-krisesenter/.

Haaland, T., Clausen, S., & Schei, B. (2005). *Vold i parforhold—ulike perspekti-ver: Resultater fra den første landsdekkende undersøkelsen i Norge (Violence in Partner Relationships—Various Perspectives: Results from the First Nationwide Survey in Norway)* (Vol. 2005:3, NIBR-report). Oslo: Norsk institutt for by-og regionforskning (Norwegian Institute for Urban and Regional Research).

Retrieved from http://www.hioa.no/Om-HiOA/Senter-for-velferds-og-arbeidslivsforskning/NIBR/Publikasjoner/Publikasjoner-norsk/Vold-i-parforhold-ulike-perspektiver.

Heiskanen, M., & Ruuskanen, E. (2011). *Men's Experience of Violence in Finland*. Report nr. 71. Helsinki: European Institute for Crime Prevention and Control. Retrieved from http://www.heuni.fi/material/attachments/heuni/reports/6KGSrDN0Z/HEUNI_report_71_Mens_experiences_of_violence.pdf.

Helweg-Larsen, M., & Frederiksen, L. (2008). *Vold mod mænd i Danmark—Omfang og karakter—2008 (Violence Against Men in Denmark—Extent and Nature—2008)*. Minister for Equality and Statens Institut for Folkesundhed (National Institute of Public Health), Syddansk University, Denmark. Retrieved from http://findresearcher.sdu.dk/portal/files/3552/2929_-_Vold_mod_m_nd_i_Danmark.pdf.

Holmberg, C., Stjernqvist, U., & Sörensen, E. (2005). *Våldsamt lika och olika: om våld i samkönade parrelationer* [Violence Equal and Unequal—Violence in Cohabiting CouplesStockholm]. Stockholms universitet, Centrum för Genusstudier.

Lövestad, S., & Krantz, G. (2012). Men's and Women's Exposure and Perpetration of Partner Violence: An Epidemiological Study from Sweden. *BMC Public Health, 12*(1), 945.

Nybergh, L., Taft, C., Enander, V., & Krantz, G. (2013). Self-Reported Exposure to Intimate Partner Violence Among Women and Men in Sweden: Results from a Population-Based Survey. *BMC Public Health, 13*(1), 845–858.

Pape, H., & Stefansen, K. (Red.). (2004). *Den skjulte volden? En undersøkelse av Oslobefolkningens utsatthet for trusler, vold og seksuelle overgrep (The Hidden Violence?: A Study of the Vulnerability to Threats, Violence and Sexual Assault of Oslo's Population)*. Report 2004:1. Oslo: Nasjonalt kunnskapssenter om vold og traumatisk stress (The Norwegian Centre for Violence and Traumatic Stress Studies). Retrieved from https://www.nkvts.no/rapport/den-skjulte-volden-en-undersokelse-av-oslobefolkningens-utsatthet-for-trusler-vold-og-seksuelle-overgrep/.

Plauborg, R., & Helweg-Larsen, R. (2012). Partnervold mod mænd i Danmark (Partner Violence Against Men in Denmark). University of Syddanske. Statens institutt for Folkesundhed (National Institute of Public Health). Denmark. Retrieved from https://www.sdu.dk/da/sif/publikationer/2013/partnervold_mod_maend_i_danmark.

Schütt, N. M. H., Frederiksen, M. L., & Helweg-Larsen, K. (2008). Unge og kærestevold i Danmark: En landsdækkende undersøgelse af omfang, karakter og følger af vold blandt 16-24-årige med fokus på vold i kæresteforhold. (Violence Among Young People in Denmark: A Nationwide Survey Investigating the Extent, Nature and Consequences of Violence Among 16–24-Year-Olds with a Focus on Violence in Intimate Relationships). Copenhagen: University of Syddansk. Statens Institut for Folkesundhed (The National Institute of Public Health). Retrieved from http://findresearcher. sdu.dk/portal/files/3553/2885_-_Unge_og_k_restevold_i_Danmark.pdf.

Storberget, K., Bråten, B., Rømming, E., Skjørten, K., & Aas-Hansen, A. (Red.). (2007). *Bjørnen sover. Om vold i familien (The Bear Sleeps: On Violence in the Family)*. Oslo: Aschehoug & Co.

Thoresen, S., & Hjemdal, O. K. (2014). *Vold og voldtekt i Norge: En nasjonal forekomststudie av vold i et livsløpsperspektiv (Violence and Rape in Norway: A National Prevalence Study of Violence in a Lifespan Perspective)* (Vol. 1/2014, Report (Nasjonalt kunnskapssenter om vold og traumatisk stress: publication) (The Norwegian Centre for Violence and Traumatic Stress Studies)). Oslo: Nasjonalt kunnskapssenter om vold og traumatisk stress. (The Norwegian Centre for Violence and Traumatic Stress Studies). Retrieved from https://www.nkvts.no/rapport/vold-og-voldtekt-i-norge-en-nasjonal-forekomststudie-av-vold-i-et-livslopsperspektiv/.

Open Access This chapter is licensed under the terms of the Creative Commons Attribution 4.0 International License (http://creativecommons.org/licenses/by/4.0/), which permits use, sharing, adaptation, distribution and reproduction in any medium or format, as long as you give appropriate credit to the original author(s) and the source, provide a link to the Creative Commons licence and indicate if changes were made.

The images or other third party material in this chapter are included in the chapter's Creative Commons licence, unless indicated otherwise in a credit line to the material. If material is not included in the chapter's Creative Commons licence and your intended use is not permitted by statutory regulation or exceeds the permitted use, you will need to obtain permission directly from the copyright holder.

4

Men's Experience of Intimate Partner Violence

In this chapter we will hear about 18 men's experiences with partner violence. These men are between 22 and 66 years of age and have experienced various forms of partner violence. Six of these men come from immigrant backgrounds; the others are ethnic Norwegians. As mentioned earlier, this interview study is, in many ways, a visibility project, since there are few substantial qualitative studies which investigate in depth men's experiences of violence in intimate relationships. Through autobiographical interviews and an interpretive phenomenological analytical approach, we wanted to give room to the men's own voices. The chapter raises the following questions: How do men describe the violence to which they are exposed? In what social contexts does this violence occur? How do men perceive their experiences of violence? And how are their lives affected by such violence and conflict?

Who Are These Men?

Most of the Norwegian men in our sample have more than three years of university or college education. Those from other ethnic backgrounds have a more mixed educational profile: several of them are very young

© The Author(s) 2019
M. I. Lien, J. Lorentzen, *Men's Experiences of Violence in Intimate Relationships*,
Palgrave Studies in Victims and Victimology,
https://doi.org/10.1007/978-3-030-03994-3_4

and have little formal education. Eight of the men have used the services of various family protection offices around the country. Most of their contact was in relation to mandatory family mediation. Nine men have taken up the offer of accommodation at two crisis centres in Norway. The last group of men were recruited through staff at these centres. The other participants were recruited via social media and with the help of staff members of two other support services.

Three of the eighteen men have experienced violence from gay partners. One of the gay men is Norwegian, the other two are of foreign origin. One of the participants from the crisis centre has not experienced violence from a partner, but grew up in a violent home. The other participants have experienced violence from a female partner. The female perpetrators come from both Norwegian and foreign backgrounds, although there is a predominance of women with foreign backgrounds in our material. This is due in part to the fact that we have consciously recruited male victims of violence from ethnic backgrounds. However, it is not the perpetrators of violence or its causes on which we aim to throw light.

In 2015 a Norwegian report was published entitled *Menn på krisesenter* (*Men at Crisis Centres*; Grøvdal and Jonassen 2015). This formed an important starting point for our study. The majority of the men in Grøvdal and Jonassen's study have a Norwegian ethnic background, which is why it was important for us to recruit men of immigrant background, in particular since this group has made increasing use of Norwegian crisis centres in recent years. In Norwegian and Nordic contexts, research into immigrant men's experiences of violence in intimate relationships is almost non-existent. The immigrant men we have interviewed in this study have all experienced physical violence as children. Some also experienced sexual abuse by neighbours while growing up in their country of origin.

To What Kind of Violence Are They Exposed?

The men have been subjected to milder as well as severe physical violence, psychological violence and threats, material violence and varying degrees of sexual harassment. One suffered life-threatening physical injuries that required extensive treatment. For the other men, the physical violence consisted of having hard objects thrown at them, being pushed, hit, scratched or kicked. Two of the men have been subjected to more occasional and so-called milder forms of psychological and/or physical partner violence. These incidents of violence have occurred in situations in which the couple were engaged in a heated discussion and are therefore of a more episodic nature.

Three of the men who were subjected to physical violence reported that they used force to hold their violent partner back. These situations are described by the men who were trying to stop the woman from harming herself, or who were acting in self-defence. A recurring theme here is that these men have made a strong decision not to use violence, a matter to which we return later in this book.

At the time of the interviews, one man was still living in a relationship marked by frequent conflict and various forms of violence. The other men had ended their relationships, and seven had experiences of violence that dated back more than five years. The majority of the men interviewed have been in therapy, which no doubt explains their ability to reflect on the effect their experiences of violence have had on their perception of themselves, and the psychological consequences of this violence on their lives.

As further discussed later in this chapter, it is without doubt the psychological violence in the form of systematic degradation, ridicule, sabotage of contact with children and so on which is most manifest, and the combination of anger, aggression, control and psychological terror is a common theme in most of the interviews. The fact that our sample consists of men from such different backgrounds ensures a rich variety in the stories about men's experience of violence in intimate relationships. We try in our analysis to bring visibility to the diversity of these experiences of violence and its consequences. We describe the context in which the violence occurs, the psychological effects it has on men's ability to function in everyday life, and how they perceive themselves as victims. Through these qualitative interviews we wanted to find out more about how the phenomenon of violence functions, and it is therefore important to be attentive to any stories that break with previous stereotypical ideas about violence.

Childhood Experiences of Violence

It is well documented in a number of studies that people who experience violence in childhood and adolescence are more vulnerable to becoming victims of violence later in life (Andersson et al. 2014; Thoresen and Hjemdal 2014; Simmons et al. 2014). In the survey *Vold og voldtekt i Norge* (*Violence and Rape in Norway*), the authors emphasise that they cannot identify the exact mechanisms at work that could explain the link between suffering violence as a child and later as an adult. In other Norwegian studies a connection has been found between partner violence and other violence, and in the first nationwide survey in Norway, *Vold i parforhold* (*Violence in Partner Relationships*), it states that "it has been found that those subjected to violence from someone other than their partner are also at greater risk of being exposed to violence from their partner" (Haaland et al. 2005, p. 50). Pape and Stefansen (2004) find similar trends in the Norwegian survey *Den skjulte volden?* (*The Hidden Violence?*). It must be emphasised, however, that the precise effects vary in these different studies.

Half the men we interviewed have either been hit by their parents or stepparents or have been bullied at school. There is a significant quantity of research that aims at understanding the relationship between risk factors and the perpetration of physical violence and victimisation. As far as the relationship between childhood violence and adulthood is concerned, we know from previous research that there is a statistical link between being the victim of violence in childhood and the risk of being subjected to violence in adulthood. The Norwegian prevalence study *Vold og voldtekt i* Norge (*Violence and Rape in Norway*; Thoresen and Hjemdal 2014) reveals clear trends towards multi-victimisation; about the link between being exposed to physical abuse as a child and as an adult Thoresen and Hjemdal state: "there was a significant increase in the prevalence of violence in adulthood in respondents who had experienced violence or sexual abuse during childhood" (p. 117). This relationship is stronger for those who, as children/teenagers, have been subjected to sexual assault than those who have been subjected to physical violence.

We therefore wanted to investigate whether any of the men in our sample had previous experiences of violence in childhood. Approximately half of the men were victims of violence in childhood. The other participants report having a secure and normal upbringing with few problems. In what follows we present some of the men's early experiences. Later in this chapter we will see some of these early experiences in relationship to the violence experienced in adulthood and how these men reflect on their own vulnerability.

Fredrik

Fredrik (53) describes serious and extensive sexual abuse from a male baby-sitter in childhood. His father disappeared from his life when he was a year old and he grew up with his mother. Despite being short of money, his mother was a resourceful woman who supported him in his school work and other activities. Fredrik says that his mother was always very concerned about him, but had to work a great deal to support the family. It was over a period of three years from the age of 7 when his mother was out of the house a lot that a male babysitter was abusing him. This serious abuse went on regularly until he was about 10 years old. It was only when Fredrik suddenly became mute one day that his mother realised that something was wrong and he told her about the abuse. His mother dismissed the babysitter, but did not take any action with any support organisations or with the police, and Fredrik grew up without ever talking to anyone else about the abuse. In his interview, he says that he felt he had a wound and a "deep hole" in him. He did not understand why his mother did not want to talk about what had happened or seek help. He describes himself as being a timorous child at elementary school, and says his teenage years were marked by enormous insecurity and eventually frequent sexual relations with both sexes. Fredrik was caught up in a cycle of ambivalence, fearful of intimate contact while being drawn to sexual experimentation:

> *You can develop a kind of hyper-sexuality even after abuse. Mine was a youth filled with lots of experimentation with both sexes. Some of which I'd rather have been spared. At the same time as being extremely scared, I went and did this.*

Fredrik expresses feelings of shame for this period of sexual experimentation. In childhood and adolescence, he developed ambivalent feelings for his mother because of her failure to help him deal with the abuse and trauma he had suffered. When, as a young man, he plucked up the courage to call a sexual abuse helpline, he was advised that they were unable to offer help to abused men:

> *She was not emphatic and said that they only dealt with sexual abuse against girls and women and that I mustn't contact them about my problems. ... I sat at home and wanted to take my own life.*

Fredrik's story is in many ways a story of revictimisation and of traumatic events that were never dealt with. He lost trust in the mother whom he loved. The story of abuse continues into his relationship with the woman he married and with whom he had children. As we will return to later, life with his wife followed a pattern of harassment, emotional abuse and episodes of physical abuse for long stretches at a time. He blamed himself both for allowing this to happen to him and for his inability to get out of the relationship before it had major consequences, for both his children and him.

Tor

Tor (66) grew up in the 1950s with his parents and one sister who was slightly older than him. He describes his childhood as difficult and turbulent, because his mother subjected both the children and their father to serious physical and psychological violence. The children witnessed their father being hit, humiliated and harassed, making Tor afraid and insecure:

> *I particularly remember a time when my mother kicked my father in the crotch so he fell down on the kitchen floor. He lay there writhing in pain, he curled up, with his huge hands clutching his crotch. We stood there terrified and watched, my sister and me. I was only eight years old at the time, but I remember it as though it was today.*

His mother also hit and kicked the children, afterwards comforting them and drying their tears. Tor reports that there were periods when his mother lost control completely and became very aggressive. Once she ran after him and rammed his head between the door and the wall. On another occasion, she pushed him down onto the bed and almost throttled him before his father came to his rescue. Tor thought she actually wanted to kill him.

Tor did badly at school. His parents got divorced when he went to primary school and, despite the fact that the mother's violence was known to child protection and social services, she got custody of Tor and his sister. Tor was terrified of his mother and wanted to live with his father. He found it very traumatic when his mother won the child custody case and he was forced to live with her. Later, when Tor's mother packed her cases one day and left the family home, his father was given responsibility for the care of both children. After this, Tor's everyday life improved, marked by caring and attention from his father. In his interview Tor describes feeling bitter towards a care system that almost broke both the children and their father.

Tor did well at school and went on to complete a prestigious education. But he says that his childhood experiences left deep marks, and he still struggles with uncomfortable memories and pain as a result of his mother's abuse. Witnessing such serious violence between his parents resulted in trauma. On several occasions during his childhood, Tor feared that his mother might actually succeed in killing him. Later in life she said she felt no remorse for the pain she had inflicted on the family. When Tor divorced his wife, and she took his child and moved to another city, his childhood traumas resurfaced.

Harald

Harald (43) grew up with his parents and two siblings. His mother stayed at home until he reached high-school age. His parents did not have the best relationship, although their arguments did not lead to violence. But Harald emphasises that he often felt insecure because he could never fully comprehend his parents' reactions to things:

It was about manipulation or the use of a bad conscience as a way of bringing children up. The demand to behave—linked to you feeling bad if you thought you'd done something wrong.

Harald grew insecure and regularly struggled with a bad conscience without quite knowing why. He felt responsible early on for everything being right at home. He says he was hyper-aware of his parents' moods and of trying to be good and dutiful: "My strategy was not to make too much of myself." Although there were lots of good things, there were so many inconsistent reactions. His mother and father often hid problems. When he was 10 years old, his grandfather came down with cancer, but his parents failed to tell Harald about his grandfather's illness until after the man's death. His grandfather's death came as a shock and Harald says it gave him a sense of insecurity that he has carried with him throughout his life:

I did not get the time or understanding to absorb what had happened. Suddenly, my grandfather was dead. I didn't get to participate in the funeral either. It's fixed in my memory, this clear and difficult childhood experience.

As an adolescent he felt unattractive to girls and found it difficult to approach them. Harald says himself that this was probably because he had always been a bit socially insecure and felt unsafe in relationships. When he met his future wife as a student, he was very surprised that such a pretty young woman could have fallen in love with him: "I was so inexperienced with girls, incredibly insecure about my looks, my body, my achievements and intellect." It soon revealed itself that his young girlfriend was self-harming. After a while she also became bad tempered and violent towards him, both verbally and physically. The violence escalated still further after they had had children. Harald stayed in the relationship for over 15 years, and even after several years of therapy he still struggles with the effects of this violent relationship.

Jon

Jon (51) grew up in a small town with his mother and father and many siblings. His parents were loving and caring towards each other, but they were always short of money and had a large number of children to take care of. Jon has suffered with psychological difficulties and anxiety for years. At the time of the interview, he was unemployed. He describes the tensions in the family he grew up in:

I grew up in a big family who did not have much money. Firstly, there were lots of us—a massive gang of us in a tiny apartment. In addition, my sister had been diagnosed with a serious mental condition, and that meant there was a fair bit of friction and high-level general stress in our family. We couldn't bring other children home. We were basically "the odd family".

It is clear from Jon's story that he was a loner, generally excluded from any friendships or relationships at school. He was close to his parents, but he also says in the interview that they were unable to cope with the children. From early on he learned to tiptoe around at home. His sister could attack her siblings physically, which caused a lot of fear and upset. He was also picked on at school, and at primary school he became the target for one of the rougher boys, who bullied him both physically and verbally. He describes serious bullying and harassment from his schoolfellows:

It was nine years of physical and mental harassment. It included everything, from trying to drown me, hitting me, kicking and bullying me. After a while I closed up.

Jon says that he shrank in on himself and did not retaliate. He was beaten and kicked and was scared of going to school. His classmates stole his clothes during gym class and held him underwater in the swimming pool. He dropped out of high school, but went back to college later. He explains that the insecurity he experienced in childhood and adolescence made him fearful of growing up and caused social anxiety.

In his 20s he met a young woman and quickly moved in with her: "We were two vulnerable souls who found each other." It turned out that his girlfriend also had difficult past experiences and had serious problems controlling her anger. For over ten years Jon was with a woman who kicked and hit him. He has sought the help of psychologists, general practitioners and other support agencies.

As mentioned earlier, we see some differences in the childhood experiences of ethnic Norwegians and men from ethnic minorities who have gone on to experience partner violence. This may, among other things, be due to cultural differences in childrearing and views on children. Most of the six men from other ethnic backgrounds have extensive experiences of violence from childhood and, as we have seen, two of them also suffered sexual abuse. The participants from immigrant backgrounds all describe a childhood in which it was quite common for children to be hit, especially by fathers, but also teachers and other people in authority. They are reluctant to call it violence; it was so common in their experience that they saw nothing special about it. For Ali, Deo and Bashir, violence was an intrinsic part of their upbringing, both within and outside the home.

Ali

Ali (55), who came to Norway when he was an adult, describes his experiences of being hit as a child:

> Researcher: Can I ask you about your experiences of violence as a child, were you subjected to violence by mother or father?
> *Yes. Not in the hard way that you'd understand it, but because in our culture they think differently. Parents think if they use a little violence or are hard on their children, that's best for them. Yes, now and again it is. I remember that I got many slaps from my father.*
> *I thought it was normal, because if you look at my situation and others of the same age, then it was fine—I was fine. It's normal to hit kids. I didn't get any violence, but he hit me. It happened. When I'd done something he didn't like.*

Ali's experience is not unique. Several men from minority groups undercommunicate the violence they experienced in childhood, normalising or trivialising it. Being hit by parents or teachers was a part of growing up for many of these men. These are not common experiences among the ethnic Norwegian men we have interviewed, however.

Deo

The story of Deo (34) has many similarities with Ali's, also being hit by his father and his teacher. During the interview, Deo initially answers "no" to the question of whether he was subjected to violence in his childhood. When the question is repeated, he again replies in the negative, but then goes on:

> *No. They are stricter in my home country, that's usual.*
> Researcher: What do you think is usual?
> *Yes. It is usual for teachers to hit [children]. I got several injuries when I was ten years old because the teachers hit me and were very strict. There were lots of rules.*
> Researcher: How did the teachers hit [you]—with a stick?
> *Yes. They hit [me] here and they hit there [indicating on his body] and they hit my legs here too.*
> Researcher: But your mother and father then?
> *Yes. Dad hit but not Mum. Dad hit the kids, but he did not hit Mum.*

We have to ask these questions several times before the story begins to come out, and what he calls "usual" reveals itself to mean quite extensive blows to his body and head. Deo came to Norway to get married. He says that he does not want to go back to his home country despite the huge problems he has had with his wife and in-laws. He has a job and security in Norway, and if he were to return life would be extremely difficult. We will come back to this later in the chapter.

Bashir

Two of the immigrant men tell us that they were victims of sexual abuse as children, both from neighbours. Bashir (20) explains:

> *When I was about ten years old, there was a man in the neighbourhood who abused me whenever he wanted to. Afterwards everyone realised that I had been abused. They bullied me and called me names.*

This abuse had major consequences for Bashir and his family. The neighbour continued his abuse for several years and when it became known among the other neighbours, it was not the perpetrator they turned against, but Bashir himself and his family. They called him gay and when he was 15 years old, they attempted to kill him. They stabbed him in the throat with a knife. The villagers persecuted the family and finally took it out on his father:

> *I was in hospital for three months afterwards, and they rang my father and said they didn't know how things were going with his boy. Then the men who'd cut my throat drove to my father's house and killed him. Because I'm gay. They went to the house and killed him while I was in hospital.*

These childhood experiences continue to affect Bashir in many ways. He suffers from social anxiety and is afraid of even associating with people. He describes extensive harassment from the people from his home country who live in the same town as him in Norway. He has huge problems with anxiety and suicidal ideation. Bashir's case probably bears the clearest hallmarks of multi-victimisation of any in this chapter.

Daniel

Daniel (25) talks about his experience of abuse by a neighbour:

> *When I was in secondary school, I was abused by the boyfriend of a [female] friend of my mother's. This friend lived across the street. It happened in the pool. We were swimming in the pool. Me, him, his son and his daughter. His wife had called their kids in because they were going away. Then he came over to me and held me and pulled down my pants and he was already hard. Then he pushed his penis into me.*

Daniel wanted to stay in the pool because he rarely got to swim in a pool. In his interview, he dismissed the idea that it may not have been a complete coincidence that he was subjected to abuse of this nature when he was 13 years old. He came from an extremely brutal background and was exposed to extensive bullying by his peers at school. He was overweight and was bullied because his family were poor or because he wore the wrong clothes. Other kids stole or broke his things. His family lived in cramped conditions in a bad neighbourhood. He describes, as a child, having to step over people who had overdosed in the stairwell, and syringes and needles lying everywhere. There were regular shootings in the neighbourhood. Daniel grew up with a vulnerability which arguably made him a potential victim. When we ask if he told anyone about the rape, he answers:

> *No, I didn't say anything because I was afraid and … well. It was a mix of lots of things. I'd been bullied, I thought it was my fault because I—I shouldn't have been in the pool alone with him. I thought what if what if, what should I have done etc. You go over the situation in your head time after time and yes…*

As we can see, Daniel looks for answers as to why he was abused. And, like several other men we interviewed who have experienced sexual abuse, described in Chap. 6, he has lived with feelings of shame and guilt for what happened.

Bashir and Daniel both experienced a great deal of violence in childhood, and both came to Norway when they were approximately 20 years old. Their relationship to violence differs from that of the other participants; both tell their experiences without holding so much back. There is a big difference in how Bashir and Daniel talk about their experiences of violence after coming to Norway, in comparison to Ali and Deo. Both Ali and Deo under-communicate the violence they have been exposed to in adulthood, something we will see later.

Several of the men talk about much of the violence they have experienced as though it were normal. It was an everyday part of life, or something that everyone did, or simply how things were. The violence these men experienced as "normal" when they were children may have contributed to their acceptance of a life of violence as adults—at least until it became too serious to be tolerated.

Peter

Peter (44) talks about this "acceptance" of violence in another way. He was also subjected to violence and witnessed frequent quarrels and physical violence between his mother and his stepfather at home as a child. He frequently got a cuff round the ear from his stepfather, but his relationship with him could be good in periods. His stepfather took him on trips and skiing. His mother was never violent towards him, but she was hot-tempered and had an argumentative relationship with her husband. Peter says that witnessing the "battles" between them made him avoid any form of confrontation and conflict later in life:

> *I don't like discussions that lead to a tense atmosphere. I don't like it. Then I withdraw, and go in on myself.*

He has learned to be evasive and has developed behaviour patterns which mean he does not confront those who treat him badly. Instead of confronting them about their actions, he tries to understand why they are behaving in the way they are.

Peter grits his teeth and retreats rather than confronting people. In his case, and in the case of several of the other men, we see a huge ability to try to understand and show compassion for the perpetrator; to such an extent that they have managed to explain away the consequences that this violence has had on them. We will return to this later in the chapter.

Experiences of Intimate Partner Violence

We will now describe the men's experiences of intimate partner violence. First we will meet men who have been exposed to systematic violence over a period of time. There is a tendency in several of the men's stories for them to have shown a lot of consideration towards their partners who have told them about difficulties in their upbringing. The partners have, at times, been so aggressive and unstable that the men have developed strategies to please them order to avoid conflict, for example by leaving the house when there are signs of irrational aggression, or being extra friendly or quiet to dampen their partner's level of aggression.

Living with Systematic Violence over Time

Harald is one of the respondents who has lived with a violent partner for the longest. When he was divorced from his wife a few years back, it was after having gone through a 15-year relationship in which violence and conflicts were a regular occurrence. It became clear to Harald early on that his girlfriend had psychological problems: she was very temperamental and tried to harm herself several times. She had told him about experiences of abuse from her adolescence and he wanted to help her. Harald realised she needed treatment, but thought that if he only he loved her enough, she would get better. The episodes of self-harm and dramatic behaviour became more frequent after they moved in together. For periods Harald had to keep watch at night in case his girlfriend tried to harm herself. In these situations, she could attack him physically: "My explanation is that it all began with her losing control of herself. She hit, kicked and bit me. She was completely rabid."

His girlfriend's episodes of rage, self-harm and physical violence towards Harald continued, in particular after disputes or when he had done something she did not like. When Harald wanted to finish the relationship, she fell pregnant.

Harald lived in a relationship where he was bitten, scratched and punched in the face until his nose bled. His wife kicked him in the crotch and threw hard objects at him when she got angry. She threatened him with a knife. He says that he was sometimes very afraid for his life. At the same time as letting loose on him, she also harmed herself. She rowed with Harald if he had been in contact with his family. He experienced an inner chaos and had ambivalent feelings, because he felt sorry for his wife and, for sake of the children and wider family, he wanted to keep the family together. It was only after the breakup that he realised how serious his ex-wife's mental health problems had been. According to Harald, she was diagnosed with bipolar disorder before the divorce, but at the time he had not known how severe it was. He smoothed things over, hid things and tried to normalise the children's day-to-day lives.

Similarly, Tom (63) describes a pattern of harassment, humiliation, bullying and various forms of physical violence in a ten-year relationship.

He had been married to another woman previously with whom he had children. There had been no violence at all in this relationship. The two had remained good friends after the divorce. Tom says it took a long time before he understood the kind of regime he was living under with his new partner because she changed slowly, becoming more controlling over time. He noticed that something was wrong in the relationship when they moved in together. She refused to let his children come to visit and would remove his private possessions without saying anything. Letters from the bank disappeared without explanation. He says he became "slightly paranoid" because things vanished. Not until much later did he realise that his partner had been behind all this. Tom describes how he was subjected to humiliation and harassment:

> We had a party one afternoon. We had babies in arms and the neighbours had been here with their toddlers. After the visitors have gone, she says: Didn't you notice? Didn't you see that people are rolling their eyes at you? They're talking to me about you. They come to me and say that they feel sorry for me because you've got such a condescending attitude towards me.

His partner's methods worsened after the birth of their child. Tom was continually told what a bad man and father he was, and that he was incapable of taking care of the child properly. He was frequently told that their mutual friends thought that he behaved weirdly and whined all the time:

> I remember we went for a walk once. She said that I shouldn't contact two of our male friends anymore because they were totally fed up with all my whining. Their wives had told her that their husbands would rather not be with me. We'd go to a birthday party, and when we got home she'd say people were nodding to each other and exchanging knowing glances because I was behaving so weirdly.

Over time, Tom began to doubt himself and felt that he was never clever enough verbally or cognitively in conversations. He says he never knew who his friends were or what other people thought about him. Tom became troubled and confused and says he lost his grip on everyday life: "Something in me snapped. There had been many such episodes, of

humiliation and insults. I locked myself in the bathroom and screamed."
He regularly went off in the middle of the night to escape the problems
and so the kids would not wake up. Occasionally he took his duvet with
him and slept in the car.

Serious Harm

Tom has also experienced serious physical violence that led to injuries.
When their child was about a year old, his partner threatened him with
an object for the first time. They were meant to have friends for dinner
and prepare the food in the kitchen. When he contradicted her about
something, she stabbed him in the face with a knife and accused him of
never contributing to the household. We asked Tom if he could predict
when his partner would become aggressive:

*Yes. I could. When the vacuum cleaner began to go at least once a day and there
was lots of unnecessary house cleaning. Then I knew something was in the air.
Perhaps the cleaning was a way of channelling her anger, I don't know. But I
learned to see the signs. The intense gaze and dark eyes. Then she'd close in on
herself. Nothing but commands came out [of her]. Then she'd start slamming
the doors.*

When his partner began to slam doors, Tom would go around the
house trying not to say or do anything that could irritate her.

Once his partner went into a fury when Tom returned home from a
Christmas party. He had had some aquavit to drink and was slightly tipsy.
When he came home at one o'clock in the morning, he got a surprise:

*Just as I get in the door, I hear someone come raging down the stairs. She stands
in the hallway and yells at me to get out. I'm saying it's okay and turn to go.
Then she catches me from behind so I fall backwards and all I can remember is
a bang when my head hits the ground. I'm lying on the floor in foetal position—I was a bit drunk too of course. Bit by bit I get back on my feet and see
myself in the mirror. There's blood all over my face and down my shirt. I have
a big cut in my head. I stagger into the bathroom and lock the door. Then she
left and went to bed.*

During his interview, Tom describes several similar incidents of physical and emotional abuse by his former partner. In one case, her 10-year-old son stands in the dark and kicks him in the face as he is coming up the stairs. Later the child is very upset and cries about the event.

But in Tom's story, there is no parallel narrative about a woman who has had bad childhood experiences or is battling with a psychiatric diagnosis. Tom's former partner was well liked at work and had a good network of friends and neighbours. He thinks she was (and is) very talented socially. This was one of the reasons why he did not tell his friends about her behaviour behind the four walls of their home.

Peter's (second) wife subjected him to various forms of violence, including economic and material violence. It started with her using his credit card and buying "stupid things just to spend money", as well as taking a knife and cutting the sofa and making knife marks on the living room wall. She also began harming herself and breaking his things. Peter explains her entire behaviour thus: "she provokes me something rotten. It's like she wants to drive me to breaking point."

Of the episode that eventually led him to leave and move to the crisis centre, he says:

> She behaves exactly as she wants, because she knows I won't do anything. After a while she got physical, she was harming herself, so we began to fight, and then she started to hit me. She hit me right in the face with her fist. Once she nearly strangled me. When I was at the doctor's a few days later, I mentioned it to the doctor because it hurt to swallow. She'd squeezed my throat that hard. The doctor asked me what had happened. I said my wife had put her hands round my throat. The doctor said he couldn't feel anything [wrong], but that he was sure it was painful. Then we got to the problem I'd gone there with. Originally she'd threatened me with—instead of threatening to hurt herself, then she started threatening me with a knife. She did this twice. With the knife in her hand. She was standing there boiling baby bottles, and once she went to pick up the saucepan full of boiling water and came over with it and threatened me that if you don't do this or that, I'll throw this over you. Then I thought, God Almighty, this is getting too crazy. I can't go on like this.

The result was that Peter left home and "wandered around the city and shopping mall until six or seven in the evening". He did not know what to do or where to go, but on the internet on his phone he found a crisis centre, where he stayed for several weeks.

The men we interviewed who attended a crisis centre because they themselves felt that the violence had gone too far had all been subjected to partner violence except one: Carlos (22), who came to stay at the crisis centre with his entire family when they fled his mother's violent partner. Since Carlos was over 18, he was obliged to stay in the men's section. Carlos's story is different from the others, in that he had not been exposed to violence from a *partner*, but was part of a household where violence and anger were commonplace, right into adulthood. We will return to Carlos's story later. He displays a tendency which we find in many of the men—a huge capacity throughout long periods of his life to take care of others.

Psychological Control

We have previously highlighted Johnson's (2008) distinction between the typologies of situational violence and intimate terrorism, and how Johnson argues that physical superiority and threats of or actual physical violence lead to the (male) partner controlling and dominating the other. In several of the stories of partner violence perpetrated by women, it is not the threat of physical violence that controls men, but that women have psychological dominance and exert control in the form of systematic harassment and humiliation.

Filip (33) is an example of the devastating effects that harassment and humiliation can have when they occur in a love relationship. Filip's story has parallels with Tom's. At the time of the interview, he is divorced from his wife. According to his description she is well liked, has a large network and is a resourceful woman in many ways.

Filip was subjected to emotional violence in the form of frequent humiliation and ridicule. He had no experience of either physical or psychological violence before his early 20s, when he met a woman four years older than him. Early on in the relationship it emerged that she could at times be destructive and aggressive. Filip was very in love with her and wanted the relationship to succeed. The problems worsened after two or three years of their being together. After their first child was born, she often went out on the town and met other men. She could be gone for whole nights at a time, without Filip knowing where she was. He explains that he loved her and became insecure and nervous when she left without telling him where she was. He describes how he experienced the situation when his wife came home in the morning:

> *What was worst was when she tells me everything. She comes home, for example, at half past seven in the morning. This is after the children are born. Later on in the day she tells me about what she's done. And it's like she's not shy, there's no embarrassment or shame or anything, but it's with a glint in her eye and this eager expression in her face—like, how's he going to react to this? A kind of hungry glow. It got disgusting, really disgusting, and that's how it was every time. So I got the feeling that she got a kick out of seeing me suffer.*

The latent threat that his wife could disappear and meet other men exhausted Filip. He describes how his anxiety began to take over: What was wrong with him? Why was she doing this to him and to the children? His wife often looked right through him, as if he were not there, when they were in the same room. She did not answer his questions or laughed when he declared his love to her. Filip felt that his wife undermined him by ignoring him and criticising him. He says he became unsure of himself and started to suffer from social anxiety. During his interview, he says that he does not dare to meet women now because he feels such anxiety about being judged, and is terrified of being rejected.

Tom became seriously ill just before the family was due to go on a trip abroad. The doctor advised him to cancel the holiday due to his general poor health. When Tom told his wife that it was unlikely he would be able to travel, she was furious and refused to let him stay at home:

> *She jumped on me, not physically, but verbally. She screamed at me saying I was weak and that I'd let the doctor control me. I was completely beaten down and went on the trip anyway. The next day I became acutely ill and had to go back home.*

Tom, Filip and Harald have all experienced psychological control in their marriages. All three of them did what they thought their wives expected of them to avoid trouble. It is not the physical violence or the threat of violence here that causes these men to feel anxiety or have other psychological reactions. Aggression and control are exerted through harassment, often combined with threats to take the children away from them or to report them for violence.

A recurring feature in the stories of men who have experienced intimate partner violence from women is that they regularly experience feelings of guilt without knowing quite why. As we will return to later in this chapter, eroded self-esteem and fear of doing and/or saying something wrong are common consequences of living with conflict and violence.

Fredrik is an example of a man whose self-esteem has been eroded after many years of experiencing serious emotional abuse and the use of control strategies. He says that he often had the uncomfortable feeling that his wife was never satisfied with him as a partner and the life they lived together. He believes that she took her own worries and stress out on him. He was never good enough, neither as a husband nor as a father. Before he left for a work trip, his wife would threaten him, saying there was no guaranteed that she and the kids would be there when he got back. Walking on tiptoe and trying to curb his wife's aggression by weighing his words carefully and being extra friendly and kind became one of Fredrik's strategies.

Fredrik says he carried a certain amount of insecurity because he was subjected to sexual abuse as a small boy. When they were discussing things, his wife would humiliate him by attacking him where he was at his most vulnerable. He explains how she exposed him to humiliation and harassment:

I felt like a shit, and that I was never good enough. I felt like that throughout the relationship. She compared me to my mates, saying that they probably had a stronger sex drive than me. … Because I'd been abused, and I'd had lots of partners before her, she reckoned I should be grateful that anyone wanted me.

Fredrik's wife often accused him of being unfaithful and looking at other women. She thought there was something wrong with him since he constantly tried to attract other people's attention. She threw wet towels in his face, wrecked things and threw knives, but Fredrik emphasises that it was the humiliation, the ridiculing of him as a partner and father and the sexual harassment that were the most devastating. He says that his wife had complete psychological dominance over him during certain periods:

> *I was cracking up and I got totally desperate. Once I tried to jump out of the car when it was moving. I couldn't bear anymore. She kept on and on at me with accusations and threats. I wasn't safe in my own home.*

Filip and Harald reported in similar terms how they broke down after enduring "floods" of humiliation and harassment. Sometimes they feel so low that they try to take their own lives.

In the Norwegian report *Menn på krisesenter* (*Men at Crisis Centres*), researchers conclude that men exposed to systematic violence from partners have many of the same needs as women with similar experiences (Grøvdal and Jonassen 2015). The men presented in the report express that they fear more violence and experience shame. They are worried about the future welfare of the children, while also caring about the perpetrator of the violence. Our survey confirms some of these findings. We too find various forms of violence and shame being inflicted, combined with men's enormous concern for the children and also for the violent partner. The men try to protect both themselves and those who perpetrate the violence, until this proves impossible and they turn to the crisis centre for help.

Seen in the context of Johnson's distinction between situational partner violence and intimate terrorism, most of the men in our study are subject to intimate terrorism. These acts of violence are part of a pattern that governs the relationship. It comprises a combination of aggressive and controlling behaviours, threats, put-downs and other forms of psychological terror combined with various forms of physical violence and, in some cases, sexual violence. It is the persistent and repetitive nature of these experiences that characterises this violence. Most of the men we interviewed from the crisis centres focus a great deal on the final violent episode which forced them onto the streets, to move out and finally go to a crisis centre. But this final episode of violence, and their reactions to it, can only be understood when viewed in the context of the violence meted out by the partner over an extended period of time.

Intimate terrorism is characterised by a partner exercising physical and psychological violence which suppresses the freedom of the autonomous subject to live in an equal relationship. Interviews with the men in our study indicate that it is not the fear of physical violence that drives the control regime, but rather psychologically controlling behaviour or fear of trouble, harassment and of losing contact with children.

Using the Child

The fathers in our sample say they have been frightened of losing contact with their children. Albert (33) is one of those we interviewed who has been subject to relatively minor attacks. Albert's ex-wife was never physically violent towards him, but worked systematically to sabotage his relationship with the children. He says that he learned to be hyper-sensitive to his ex-wife's moods after the breakup to avoid her putting a spoke in the wheels when he was going to have the children. She regularly changed her plans just before he was going to pick up the children and refused him permission to take them on holidays that they had planned long in advance. At one time she even contacted the child welfare office and accused him of kidnapping one of the children. Her new husband has also been verbally threatening towards Albert in social situations, in the presence of the children.

One of the men represented here has never lived with the mother of the child he had in mature years. His story illustrates a particularly serious example of a psychological abuse and control strategy used by mothers over fathers who are in a weaker legal position as regards the child than either married or cohabiting fathers. Andreas (55) describes having continual problems with an ex-girlfriend who limits and controls his movements with his son. He met this woman through common friends. Some months after they had got together, she began to behave aggressively without cause:

There was this sudden violent need to be in control. Detailed planning, almost to the minute. She could flare up if it didn't go quite as she'd planned. Eventually I felt that our relationship had no future. Just when I'd decided to end the relationship, she calls and tells me she's pregnant.

Andreas decided to make the best out of the situation. He very much wanted to take part in the responsibility for his son's upbringing despite the relationship being over, but his ex-girlfriend would have nothing to do with him:

> *After the birth she was totally weird. She became a lioness who was constantly on the look out. I wasn't allowed to change the baby's nappy. I wasn't allowed to put him to bed. I was barely allowed to hold him, but I thought all this would pass when our son got a bit bigger.*

This constant watchfulness over the father and son did *not* pass. When Andreas tried tentatively to suggest to her that he might have regular contact with his son, the mother refused. Access based on any usually acceptable structure was out of the question. Andreas describes how his movements with his son were controlled:

> *A stopwatch was set when I went out with the pram. If I wasn't back after 45 minutes, then all hell let loose, total panic. She yelled at me and raged and went hysterical. She couldn't control herself, got very angry and yelled and screamed at me. I was screamed at a lot, and that affected me very strongly because I wasn't used to that sort of thing.*

It was revealed after a while that their son had a psychological developmental disorder and needed special care and educational support. In order to be around more, Andreas moved into a house close to his ex-girlfriend, but not long afterwards she took her son and moved in with her parents many miles away. The courts had awarded him contact every other weekend and once a week, but this never materialised. His ex-girlfriend systematically sabotaged the contact. He would travel to meet his son feeling uneasy and fearful as to whether he would be able to spend time with him or not. One afternoon when Andreas came to pick up his son, he was also threatened by other family members:

> *She and her family had obviously made a plan, an ambush attack. When I came in the door the father of my ex-girlfriend was sitting there filming me on a video-recorder as I walked in and picked him up. My son is strongly impacted*

by his diagnosis and is socially reticent. It wasn't as though he jumped up to meet me like other children do. Inside, his grandmother sat there yelling at me: "Look how he's wrecking the boy!" My son was very frightened. It was a completely absurd situation. I didn't get to take my son with me. Things became too much for me after this episode. I went into a depression and stopped asking for any contact because it was all so mad.

Like many other men, Andreas never uses the word violence when referring to his experiences. "Crazy" and "mad" are the words used more frequently to describe what they have been subjected to. We will return to this later in the chapter.

After a while, Andreas agreed to his ex-partner's proposal of contact under her supervision. He could take his son on holiday or to his house or to visit his family, provided that his ex-partner was present. Andreas has decided to live with this solution to protect his son and himself.

Both Albert and Tor were threatened with being taken to court if they did not agree to the contact agreements that their ex-partners sketched out prior to their meetings with family protection. Tor came under pressure from his ex-wife during negotiations about care and residence, and ended up paying her a huge amount of money to share the care. She said that if he refused, she would go to court. Christian (28) was also threatened in the same way by his ex-wife.

The desire to be a modern father who was present for his children clearly emerges in Andreas's story. The person who carried out his interview felt that the sorrow and pain he had sustained were palpable. He was not allowed to change his son's nappies because the mother expressed a fear that he might abuse the boy. Threats, tirades and the casting of aspersions became an integral part of any meeting. He was caught in a game of control mechanisms. He was willing to adapt to a highly controlling regime in order to spend as much time as possible with his son. Both Andreas's and Tor's narratives are stories of a lost fatherhood and of various forms of second-wave abuse in the institutions they have come into contact with (Corbally 2015, p. 3120). While Andreas suffers in silence, Tom adopted the same methods as the mother. Becoming desperate, he took his child back to his home and refused to return her to her mother because she had moved home without consent. After several years of very serious conflict, he lost all contact with the child.

Excessive Control Exercised over Daily Life

Peter explains that the violence began with his wife's jealousy of his children from a previous relationship: of his spending too much time with them, being too affectionate and sitting next to them, instead of with her on the couch. His wife's jealousy eventually resulted in more controlling behaviour, both control of his relationship with the children, and also of when and how he should communicate with their mother. Any messages to his ex-wife had to go through his new wife's phone, in addition to her dictating what he could write. There should be no niceties like "hello" or "how are things".

Deo's story comprises many of the same elements, although the control exercised over his life is even greater. Deo came to Norway to get married, but it was a couple of years after his arrival that his wife began to quarrel with him, threatening him, blaming him for things and generally taking control of his life. She inflicted injuries on him several times, scratched him, threw things on the floor and at him: "threw lamps and the like in the bedroom". She also controlled his spending, and eventually also brought her family in to decide with her how Deo should use his money and time. Deo found this very humiliating and cried several times during the interview:

> *They want to look at my finances, it's horrible. It's sad. My dad has never looked at them. Friends of hers have also done that. I don't like to live because … my wife knows how much I earn and how [much] I send home. My wife knows everything. I often showed my wife my account and she knows how [much] money I send. I don't have any secrets, none.*

His wife controls his life in almost every detail. She decides when Deo can go out and regularly threatens to send him back to their homeland:

> *She travels back to our home country, but I'm not allowed to go out or visit friends. It's not allowed. She is strict. She can travel. But I cannot go out and she wants me to tell her who I've talked to and who I've called. When get our pay at work we get together and go for a beer, I don't drink. I went once, but my wife wouldn't let me go the next time. I'm just at home, I can't do anything, I clean the house and clear the snow and go to work. No fresh air.*

In the end, the threats from both his wife and her family are so great that Deo seeks help. He is encouraged by people he meets in adult education to contact the crisis centre, and he moves in.

Deo is subjected to enormous social control and violence from both his wife and his in-laws in Norway and her wider family back in their homeland. The money he earns and his car keys are confiscated, his movements are controlled, and his wife's brothers demand insight into his finances. His wife often calls him several times a day when he is at work, which creates difficulties for him with colleagues. If he does not do what his wife and her family say, they threaten to send him home. This is an unbearable idea for him since the shame would be horrendous, nor does he know what his wife's family (and his own family) would do to him if he was returned.

Situational Partner Violence

Three of the men in this sample have experienced violence that has come and gone in periods, and can be characterised as situational couple violence based on Johnson's (2008) definition. Although the men describe repeated episodes of physical, material and psychological violence, it is not certain that their partners have psychological control over them or that they systematically dominate them. Christian's wife was only physically violent when they had arguments. She was from Latin America and they got married quite soon after meeting so that she could get a residence permit. Christian says that he was very in love with her. Their relationship did not go well, however, and Christian eventually got the feeling that she was not really in love with him, but was just using him. She often threatened to move out and she could stay away for several days without his knowing where she was. She lied to him and went with other men behind his back.

There was a great deal of conflict in the relationship between Christian and his wife, and he is one of the men who explains that on some occasions he used his physical superiority to defend himself. He and his wife had no children and he has not sought help from any agencies. On two occasions, the police arrived at the door because of the noise. Once,

Christian called the police himself because his wife had bitten him and drawn blood. The police came and took his wife to the station for questioning. The police thought Christian should file a report on the incident, but he did not want to because he felt sorry for her. He also felt that he had started the argument by trying to take her mobile phone from her. On another occasion, the police came to the house because the neighbours had reported a disturbance. Christian's wife had kicked him and thrown a candlestick at him, and he had kicked her in the thigh in self-defence. When the police arrived, the woman had marks on her thigh and he had a bruise on his forehead. The police drove her immediately to the crisis centre.

In the case of Christian and his wife, the violence is in part mutual, but the psychological pressure and harassment to which she subjected Christian led to him being unable to sleep and losing his grip on reality. He explains that friends and other networks helped him to recover after the breakup with his wife.

Erik (52) is the only man in this study who still lives with a violent wife. She originally comes from somewhere in Africa and told Erik about various physical violence and sexual abuse which took place in the family in which she grew up. His wife is only violent when she drinks alcohol and, according to Erik, she is fast developing an alcohol problem. She has broken a computer and other valuables in fits of rage. She tries to control who he sees and what he spends his time on. In arguments she has said that no one else would want him and shouted out how ugly and hopeless he is. She has also threatened to call the crisis centre and report him for being violent towards her. Afterwards she cries and says she is upset and ashamed at what she has done.

Main Breadwinner and Victim

Low income and poor educational attainments are, in themselves, risk factors for becoming the victim of violence. It is well documented in clinical trials of abused women that as a group they are often outside the world of work. Half the residents of Norwegian crisis centres are on benefits (Bufdir 2016). There are relatively large differences in terms of employment and income among the respondents in this study, but the majority are middle-class and employed. Most of the participants resemble many other Norwegian men in that they are, or have been, the main providers for their families. This, to some degree, also includes the two heterosexual immigrant men who have lived in Norway long enough to get work permits. We find an interesting ambivalence in this section of the study as regards the attitude of these men towards the traditional notion of a man as active protector and main breadwinner, and their experiences as victims of violence. They offer financial support and want to protect their wives and children, and yet they are simultaneously subjected to partner violence.

Deo had several jobs when he arrived in Norway. It was necessary for him to send money to his family and also to satisfy his wife's demands. Now he has *one* job which he really enjoys. He says his job is what gives him the will to live. He has work colleagues there and the person he calls his only friend. Outside work, he is still completely isolated and is frightened of going out.

Most men point to their work as an important anchor in their lives. Those who have had a job have managed to keep hold of it, even when this has at times been very difficult. Jonas (46) says that he had to sleep in a container for several days because his wife had thrown him out, and he was careful that no one should discover it. At other times he worked continuously to satisfy his wife's needs and demands for money, and describes how he once "ended up sleeping only a few hours a day for 14 days". The burden of providing for the family lay with these men. Their identity as men was largely linked to their being proactively involved as fathers and successful in their working lives.

Harald says that he had several jobs at times to keep the wheels turning, because his wife could not handle the workplace. In periods of increased conflict and violence he went on sick leave. This led to feelings of stress and anxiety at not managing well enough. Tom was providing for his wife who worked part-time. Being in the role of a strong and active protector for the family may have made it difficult for some of these men to see themselves as the victims of violence. Their superior economic position may also have meant that parts of the available support system, and even friends and networks, failed to notice them or identify them as victims within their relationships. But as mentioned previously, we also have examples of stories from younger men who do not have their own financial resources or any work.

It is not, these men tell us, always for economic reasons that they work longer hours in difficult periods. The majority explain that they went to work despite any physical injuries and/or the psychological pressures, and Harald, Tom and Erik all say that they spent more hours at work to escape the chaos at home.

I Am a Man and I Do Not Hit Women

None of the men interviewed reports having taken the lead in the use of physical violence against their partners. Tor and Albert have both defended themselves verbally against their ex-wives when they threatened to sabotage their contact with the children. Christian held his wife down and kicked her back when she hit him. In some cases they say they have defended themselves verbally and physically, responding with derogatory language and offensive behaviour, holding their partners back when they have attacked them, kicking out to defend themselves from being bitten and kicked, trying to lock their partner's hands, and one man says he brought his wife down to the floor to make her stop.

Arild's (43) answer to the question as to whether he himself has ever hit his partner is typical:

> Researcher: Can I ask you about the situations that became physical—did you hit her back then or were you both sort of kicking and hitting each other?
> *No, I have never hit her, but once when she went crazy and flew at me, I managed to hold her hands and knock her legs aside, very carefully and hold her on the ground for a couple of minutes, but then she was totally crazy.*

Men generally regard themselves as physically stronger and some, but far from all, use this strength to defend themselves against violence. In line with Johnson's categories of violence, we can term this form *violence resistance*; that is, a form of violence that occurs in self-defence as a response or counter-action to the systematic abuse and control behaviour of a partner (Johnson 2008). As previously mentioned, intimate terrorism is where an individual is systematically violent and controlling and the partner is not. The men we interviewed who say they defended themselves have not, so far as we have ascertained, exercised general control over their partners (Johnson 2008, p. 6).

In those cases where there is a female perpetrator of violence, the men clearly state that they regard it as unmanly to hit a woman, and hitting back has therefore not been an option. The men's attitude to violence must be seen in light of the fact that in Norway, as in many other European countries, violence towards women is a gender equality issue (Gottzén 2016). In a Swedish study of male perpetrators, Gottzén describes how violent men often exhibit shame, condemning and criticising their own actions (p. 170). Gottzén sees the shame experienced by these men in the context that abusive husbands represent a deviation that undermines the Nordic ideology of gender equality (p. 163).

The majority of the men we interviewed said that they actively distance themselves from violence in general, and that they have been brought up to believe that men should not hit women. These men regard it as an expression of strength when they do not hit their partners back. For example, Jon says: "I did not experience that it [not responding violently] threatened my identity as a man, because I think it's more manly not to hit." Harald says: "I've never identified myself with 'macho ideals' and I do not hit women."

Ali, who is from Asia, is one of the men who openly says that it is not good for a man to admit he has been hit by a woman. He also has great difficulty in talking about the physical and psychological violence to which he has been subjected. One of the reasons given by Deo for not retaliating is that he is also afraid of his own anger, that he might be triggered into being violent and injuring his wife. For men who live with a female partner, using violence as self-defence is high risk because of the difference in physical strength which often exists between women and men. One of the respondents pointed out that this was a major reason for his going to a crisis centre: he was quite simply fearful that he might retaliate and of the possible consequences of doing so, and that he might even risk killing her. Tom explained that he was terrified of finding himself in a situation where he would react to his partner's repeated provocations and end up on the front page of the local newspaper as a wife beater or killer.

There are others too who say they have been terrified of losing control and hitting back. Non-retaliation, holding out and taking responsibility for the children and family all seem to act as confirmation for them that they are proper men and fathers. Men also know that if they do retaliate, they risk not being believed and fear getting into serious trouble with the police and child welfare.

This gender relationship is not the same for those who have experienced violence from a male partner. The gay men also say they have not used violence, but we do not find the same man/woman narrative in their stories. For them the thought of hitting their partner has simply not occurred to them.

Gender Switching of Perpetrator and Victim

Another important finding is that men fear false accusations that *they* are violent. Fredrik's ex-wife threatened him with telling other people that he had hit her if he ever left her. He had no idea what the other people in the village thought of him, and grew anxious about mixing with people. He tells us that he has experienced various crises and very dangerous situations at work, but it was the war at home that broke him. These men find that women occupy a position that gives them enormous credibility with both the family and child protection services, and that it is easy for them to represent the man as the perpetrator of violence. The threat of *role switching* is expressed in different ways. For example, Filip described how his ex-wife sat in a meeting with child protection after an episode where she had thrown their youngest boy out in the freezing cold, and dismissed his story:

> *Yes. She sat there and said: Yes, but what mother could do something like that to her children? It was a rhetorical question of course. Who was going to believe that she could subject her husband and children to psychological abuse?*

Peter and Deo both describe an additional stress that complicates their relationship with their partners and the outside world still further; that is, that their wives accuse *them* of being violent. They do this by running out onto the street and shouting and screaming that they have been attacked. Deo explains:

I don't hit my wife. She often threatens me, calls the police several times. I don't hit her, but she often shouts and runs out into the street and says I'm hitting her. … I call the police and ask for help. Because my wife is attacking me and causing me injuries and running out into the street shouting, and there are lots of neighbours watching and lots of neighbours don't understand of course, because they think: he's a foreigner and he's violent. I don't like it, because they see we have a crisis. She shouts and runs into the street—I don't like that.

In similar vein, Peter says:

Yes. She's yelled and screamed and then tried to run outside. She knows how I feel about the neighbours—like what they might think or believe. You can see for yourself if she comes running out screaming—who's fault is everybody going to think it is? Mine, of course, so I'm left sitting there and everybody thinks it's me who's … and she knows that because I've told her and that's why she keeps rushing out randomly, again and again.

The men are extra vulnerable because it is easy to believe that a woman is being beaten by her husband if she runs outside screaming. Both men express a level of desperation and a huge sense of helplessness over the gendered social order to which they are subject. They have been rendered powerless and do not know how to tackle the situation. It is extremely likely, in the cases of both Peter and Deo, that the very fact that they are men subjected to violence by female partners, while their female partners protect themselves by saying that it is their husbands who are violent, has actually prolonged the violence to which they have been victim. Both express how hard it is to get anyone to believe them.

Arild experiences another variation of this switching of the violent relationship. He describes an incident when his wife had been out on the town drinking and came home with one side of her face completely smashed. She told him that she had slipped on the ice on her way home. She had big bruises on her face for four weeks. After they broke up, she told all her colleagues that Arild had been knocking her about for years, referring back to the time when she had had big bruises on her face. Arild says: "I think their reaction would be—well, I'd never have thought that of him, and you can't ever know when you're looking at things from the outside, and—she was totally black and blue and beaten up, wasn't she. I think it's dreadful."

This switching around of the violence relationship should be viewed as a significant form of psychological abuse to which men are subjected. This is a strategy available only to women, not to men, and is based on the wider society's accepted narrative about violence in intimate relationships where women are the only legitimate victims. This is a form of violence that it is difficult to imagine women being subjected to.

Minimising the Physical Violence

Men are subjected to systematic psychological, material and economic violence and controlling behaviour from their female partners. The physical violence directed against men is less systematic, but, as we have seen, over half of the men are subjected to physical violence with relatively significant potential to do damage. It has also been found that a proportion of these men are reluctant to talk much about this physical violence. Many of them begin by minimising or trivialising it, before the details gradually start to emerge and we eventually find out that they have in fact feared for their lives—which was their reason for going to a crisis centre.

It is well documented in previous prevalence studies that men living in violent relationships are subjected to less severe physical violence than women in comparable situations. As mentioned earlier, there are methodological challenges inherent in comparing prevalence studies and clinical trials, and we will not embark on any detailed discussion of gender symmetry here. However, based on the results of our interviews, it is reasonable to conclude that physical violence is under-communicated and may be far more extensive than men report. As we have seen, it took a long time before these men realised that they were victims of various forms of violence, some claiming that they did not fear the physical violence.

It is often only through quite detailed questioning, and sometimes a certain amount of persistence from interviewers, that we have revealed the physical violence and its severity. This is particularly true of those men we interviewed who came from minority backgrounds. We also see a tendency for the distance of time to impact on men's understanding of what they have been subjected to. Those men who have had a chance to look back on a violent relationship and have had therapy find it easier to recognise violent episodes.

Here we reproduce an extensive sequence from our interview with Ali, because it serves as a good illustration of the minimisation of physical violence.

Researcher: Can you describe what happened?

For example I never thought this would happen, but life is impossible to describe because we are human. Now and then something happens suddenly, and you don't understand why. Sometimes I hear that age affects and…

Researcher: Yes, but if you were to describe what concretely happened to you without interpreting it?

What happened—the other side, she only thinks about herself—because if you think about yourself, you don't listen to anyone.

Researcher: What has she done to you, in reality?

She has done it?

Researcher: What has she done?

She doesn't listen to me, or the children. Not anyone, not even to her friends.

Researcher: Can I ask you concretely—what has she subjected you to; is it physical violence or psychological violence?

Nothing.

Researcher: Nothing? No physical violence.

No.

Researcher: She hasn't hit you or kicked you?

Yes, she has, but I can't describe it as violence, no.

Researcher: Forget the word violence, just describe what actually happens?

She has thrown the key at me, yes, in my face. She was very angry and she pushed me against the door.

Researcher: Did you fall?

Yes, she's controlled me. I thought if I fell, it would be serious for me because I'm sick and I have problems with my back. Sometimes I lose the balance.

Researcher: She has pushed you?

Yes, two three times, but I…

It becomes clear later in the interview that Ali's wife has repeatedly thrown keys in his face and pushed him so hard that he has fallen. The situations he describes have been so aggressive in nature that Ali has been afraid of what might happen to him. At the time of the interview he had left the marital home and sought help at the crisis centre.

Similarly, Jonas tells us that he did not really understand that he was being subjected to systematic violence. He thought it was just an accident that he suddenly got an arm or elbow "in his face". He could not understand that she might be doing it on purpose. So for years he lived with her bashing him in the face with an arm or elbow, or throwing things at him and constantly losing her temper and screaming at him.

Tom wants to be recognised as a victim of violence while simultaneously being aware that he contributed to concealing it. He says that the shame has been unbearable and reproaches himself for not having dealt with the situation head on. Both Erik and Harald, who have been subjected to physical violence, said they were terrified that their wives might inflict serious injuries on them, but generally insist that they ought to have been able to cope with the attacks, and say they were not afraid even when knives and candlesticks were thrown at them. We see this as an under-communication of serious violence, something that should be seen in the light of ideals that suggest that men should tolerate pain and discomfort (Seidler 1997; Kimmel 2002).

As mentioned in our introduction, it is Michael P. Johnson's understanding of violence as a phenomenon and his theory that have formed the starting point for our analysis. When, in his research, Johnson (2008) decides to replace the concept of *patriarchal terrorism* with *intimate terrorism*, it is precisely because he realises that it is not only men who, out of a patriarchal ideology, commit serious violence against their female partners, but that women also commit serious and systematic violence towards their male partners. Nevertheless, there is very little in his research on how female violence unfolds and how the male victim experiences this violence in a relationship that is characterised by intimate terrorism. The interviews we have described are therefore important in improving our understanding of how intimate terrorism functions when the victim is a man.

What we find, and what is interesting in this context, is that the men discover that parts of the public support network, especially family protection and child welfare, do not recognise or see that men may be victims and/or do not understand the psychological regimes in which they find themselves.

Sexual Violence from a Male Partner

We mentioned previously that three of the men have been exposed to sexual violence. The most serious example is that of Daniel, who was repeatedly subjected to sexual abuse by his husband. He had completed his education and had a good job in his home country when he met his future partner. They became boyfriends and decided to get married and move to Norway. Daniel left his home (and his good job) and went with his partner to Norway to start a new life. His partner had never been violent towards him before coming to Norway. Shortly after their arrival, his partner getting involved in sexual practices including group sex, fisting and the use of hard drugs. Daniel did not want to participate in this, but was forced to do so. His partner became very controlling and this soon developed into physical violence, hitting him, kicking him, spitting, using a knife, locking him in and sexual abuse. Daniel says:

> He started getting violent, for example, forcing me to have sex, sometimes he hit me, pushing me onto the bed … and said he would rape me and fuck me.

Daniel does not have a permanent residence permit. His husband often threatened to tell the police stories so that they would send him out of the country. Controlling behaviour combined with manipulation and violence kept Daniel in a difficult situation, until he finally decided to call the crisis centre and moved in.

Daniel and Deo are in a particularly difficult situation due to the fact that neither of them has permanent right of residence in Norway, and their spouses threatened to get them thrown out of the country. Such threats are particularly degrading because they make them feel they have no rights. Both feel especially vulnerable and they are insecure about the framework around their own lives. The help they received from the crisis centre has therefore been particularly important. This help has contributed to the fact that they are now in the process of rebuilding their lives.

Male Vulnerability and Male Pain

Neither in popular perception nor in social research is vulnerability a trait much associated with the male role. On the contrary, research on the subject of men has generally concerned itself with men's strength and courage, or perhaps we should say men's desire to demonstrate these traits. One of the earliest studies of men and masculinities clearly revealed what was to become the main focus of men's studies. In the book *The Male Sex Role*, American sociologists Sarah David and Bob Brannon divide masculinity into four categories: *No sissy stuff* (that is, keep clear of anything that smacks of femininity), *The big wheel* (the battle for success and status), *The sturdy oak* (always strive to be tough and have control, preferably over yourself and others) and, last but not least, *Give 'em hell* (be brave, show aggression and always be ready for a fight). These categories reflect a significant level of stereotyping and some degree of irony (David and Brannon 1976). Nonetheless, many might still say that there is something in this understanding when we look at the way masculinity is presented, both as a fictional entity and in the real world.

In other research into men too, the focus is largely directed towards hegemonic manliness (Kimmel 2002). Where violence is the theme, the focus is generally on men as the perpetrators of violence and rarely on men as the victims of violence (Kimmel 2002; Gottzén 2016). In our material, however, we get an insight into male vulnerability. Men who are subjected to systematic abuse do not wish to respond to this violence with further violence, and in so doing become linked with traditional notions of masculinity. On the contrary, several of the men we interviewed expressed a will to understand their partners and show them care and love. For example, when asked why they have not reported the violence to the police, several respondents answered that they did not want to expose their partners to the consequences of such an action, be that in relation to employers or to the children or other social contexts.

Peter is one of the men who has stood by his wife for several years and helped her with her problems, despite her subjecting him to physical and mental violence for several years. Since she has obvious problems (including with self-harming), he has taken her to doctors and psychologists and tried to get the help she needs from relevant professional organisations.

Asked why he has not reported her after the episodes of serious violence, he replies that "if I report her violence it will cause her problems and have consequences for her later in her work", and that is not something he wants. That fact that she has obvious difficulties means that Peter understands her and tries to help her, with the consequence that the violence against him is in reality under-communicated.

Carlos is staying at the crisis centre because his mother has been a victim of violence for several years. He has experienced extensive violence within his family throughout childhood, yet, despite his youth, Carlos shows incredible understanding towards the perpetrators of this violence. He has intervened between his stepfather and mother several times, calmed situations that could easily have escalated, talked with his stepfather about his problems and got him to open up about his childhood experiences of sexual violence from his own father. Carlos has also postponed his education to stay at home and ensure that his mother is not subjected to further violence. Although the police and other bodies have been involved, Carlos's efforts have been crucial for the whole family. He is also among those who were both relieved and grateful to come to a crisis centre, and who greatly appreciated the support offered.

One of the questions we asked respondents was whether being a victim of violence had any significance for their identity as men. It was important to us that the men be able to reflect on their experience of themselves as men being subjected to violence, in order to challenge stereotypes of masculinity. Jonas described a psychologist whom he had visited who had little understanding of why he continued to live in a violent relationship for so long:

Researcher: You mentioned that your male psychologist said that men aren't the ones in relationships of this kind being harassed so much. But do you have any thoughts about how your identity as a man was affected by being exposed to partner violence in this way?

I know I've thought about it. What it's done to me as a man? I don't know.

Researcher: I think perhaps it's not easy to answer that, but there are certainly some set beliefs that men don't put up with that sort of thing.

I was like that too once. But it takes strength not to hit out. I've often thought that. I've used more strength both mental and physical in not hitting back. So

I haven't—what it's done to me as a man, yes, I've got an incredible amount of mental strength and I've used an incredible amount of strength in not hitting. It would have been a lot easier for me to hit her.

Jonas has thought about the relationship between masculinity and violence; more specifically, he reflects on the expectations which go with being a man in our society—he says it would have been much easier for him to hit his partner back. Nonetheless, Jonas chooses another solution; that is, not to use violence, and instead to mobilise a great deal of strength so as not to respond with violence to the extensive harassment and violence he has suffered for years. But this also leaves him extremely vulnerable, and the consequence is that he almost negates his own self in his attempt to understand and live with such violence. He frequently thinks that he would be better off dead and, looking back, Jonas sees that he almost obliterated himself entirely in his way of being.

It is essential that we reflect a little on the question of whether this violence had any impact on the victims' identity as men. For us, however, this was one of the hardest questions to put to respondents, and on listening back through the interviews afterwards we can see that we have almost shrunk back from asking it, and sometimes reformulated the question so as to avoid linking it directly to their masculinity, asking instead if the violence has had an impact on them as a person. This, in itself, says a great deal about our ideas and understanding of the notion of masculinity or manliness. It can seem that just by *asking* if this meant something to them as men, we are signalling that their masculinity has been undermined. Recognising this presumption is essential in understanding the vulnerability of masculinity.

Being the subject of violence rather than the perpetrator, being the recipient rather than the agent, being passive rather than active, can be a difficult thing for men to acknowledge. Fjell also deals with this in his book about male victims: "Men who do not defend themselves but take a passive stance represent a shift in our understanding of masculinity" (Fjell 2013, p. 139). In the case of violence, there are two conditions that make this difficult: first, a centuries-old notion of men as proactive, powerful and in control; and second, 40 years of feminist tradition that assumes that women are the sole victims of violence in intimate relationships.

Both are problematic, and both make it difficult for men to be believed by others, or even to believe it themselves, when they say that they are the victims of their partner's violence. Many of the men have not fully recognised that what they have been subjected to is indeed violence, because they have had neither the language nor the concepts to apply to it.

One of the most important aims of this study is perhaps to help to put words to the experience of these men. Commenting on men's word use in describing the violence to which they have been subjected, Fjell says: "With the exception of a few men, who during the interview reason their way to the idea that they are victims of violence, this is a term that men do not generally use. Instead, words such as 'madness', 'manipulation' and 'short-tempered'" (Fjell 2013, p. 138) come to the fore. Several of the men we interviewed only started to describe it as violence after attending the crisis centre or having therapy and talking about their experiences, thus being able to see them in a wider perspective. According to Seidler (1997), keeping their emotions in check is a widespread way for men to handle difficult life experiences. In his book *Unreasonable Men*, however, Seidler (1997) describes how men are taught to base their evaluation of themselves on external criteria: "So a gap opens up between our inner lives and outward expression that becomes difficult to overcome" (p. 135). Keeping quiet about problems becomes a form of self-protection to avoid revealing weakness (p. 135). An extremely positive finding in this study is that professional organisations and support services have started to recognise men's suffering and are willing to offer them help in reorienting themselves in their everyday lives and within society generally.

Bearing in mind the findings outlined in this chapter, it is not altogether surprising that we have relatively few in-depth answers from respondents to the question of whether violence has influenced their experience of themselves as men. Several of them say that they have not thought about it. Some say that they do not find it embarrassing or feel ashamed, while others experience it as degrading and shameful. Several think that the violence was difficult to talk about, but they have been met with understanding when they have finally opened up about it to family or friends. The most comprehensive dialogue on this theme emerged in the interview with Daniel.

Researcher: May I ask you if you've ever posed yourself questions like: why does this happen to me … and who you are as a person, as a man …

My personality changed, I used to be happy and be out with friends. Sometimes, I feel like a woman with 10 children who's stuck in a relationship because she doesn't want the kids to lose their father, something like that if you get what I mean. That I'm sacrificing something to be in this relationship with him. I realise now that I shouldn't use time on this relationship. That I should be happy and not worrying about a partner who wants to kill himself, or being forced to have sex and spat on. I asked questions like that about myself, and then I realised that this isn't how I used to be, this isn't the person I am.

Researcher: Some men have said that being beaten as a man can take away from their sense of manhood. Because this shouldn't really happen to men, as you said, when you search the internet, you generally find information about women who are subjected to violence. Is this something you've thought about?

There's some help on the internet for men too, but it's mostly offered to women. But I haven't felt less of a man because I'm quite open that this can happen to anyone. It can happen to women and to men. But if someone sees a woman hit a man on the street, people will stop and say: something's going on here, he's probably been cheating on her or something. If they see a man hit a woman— call the police!! It's true, because that's the way society is. If they see a man being hit, he's a man, he can't be hurt, he's got to be a man and just tolerate it. But for me it's the same and it doesn't make me feel less a man or whatever … no, I was open, this can happen to anyone at all. I'm not ashamed either because it happened. Because I'm gay and this kind of thing happens in relationships. Yes, it can happen.

Researcher: Maybe it's different if you're in a heterosexual relationship and you're hit by a woman, I don't know.

Yes, of course, it's another thing if you've been beaten up by your wife. That's what's hard to talk about.

The three men who have experienced violence from their male partners do not feel that this has affected their sense of self as men, even though their lives have been affected very badly by the violence to which they have been exposed. When the relationship is between a woman and a man, men appear to be affected by the heteronormative understanding of the power relationship between women and men, and in such a relationship men are not the victims of violence.

Bjerkeseth also poses questions about men's experience of themselves as men in her master's dissertation "Den mannlige offerrollen" (The Male Victim Role; 2010). Bjerkeseth does not find that violence threatens their self-esteem as men. The men she interviews define the male role as caring, attentive, characterised by openness, integrity and an ability to talk about emotions (Bjerkeseth 2010, p. 77). Bjerkeseth claims that on the one hand men tend to under-communicate and trivialise the seriousness of the violence they have been subjected to, and on the other hand they do not feel threatened by talking about it. Despite the fact that violence against men has been invisible in research, in the wider social discourse and in the historical narrative about men, it seems that men are generally able to speak openly about their own experiences of violence without defining themselves as victims.

As described earlier in this chapter, the most obvious consequences of violence are withdrawal and loneliness. Even though the men in our study do not associate this directly with their own experience of themselves as men, there seems to us to be a correlation between their desire to maintain a sense of manliness and one or more of the following:

- They do not recognise themselves as victims of systematic violence before the violence becomes life threatening.
- They keep it to themselves for a long time and think that they can handle it.
- They feel lonely and isolated.
- They withdraw from social situations and do not join in activities that they would otherwise have participated in.

In the next chapter, we will investigate the consequences that violence has had on the mental health and everyday functioning of men. In what ways do these experiences of intimate partner violence affect their lives after the violence has ceased, and how do they deal with the varying effects?

References

Andersson, T., Heimer, G., & Lucas, S. (2014). *Forekomststudien Våld och hälsa – En befolkningsundersökning om kvinnors och mäns våldsutsatthet samt kopplingen til hälsa (A Prevalence Study on Violence and Health: A Population Survey Investigating the Exposure of Women and Men to Violence and Its Links to Health)*. Nationellt centrum för kvinnofrid (National Centre for Women's Peace), NCK. Sweden: Uppsala University. Retrieved from http://nck.uu.se/kunskapsbanken/amnesguider/att-mata-vald/befolkningsundersokningen-vald-och-halsa/.

Barne-, ungdoms- og familiedirektoratet (Bufdir). (2016). Rapportering fra krisesentertilbudene 2015 (Norwegian Child, Youth and Family Directorate (Bufdir) (2016) Report of Services Offered by Crisis Centres 2015). Report 11/2016. Retrieved from https://www.bufdir.no/global/Rapportering_fra_krisesentertilbudene_2015.pdf.

Bjerkeseth, L. B. (2010). Den Mannlige Offerrollen: En Intervjustudie Av Menn Som Opplever Vold Fra Kvinnelig Partner (The Male Victim Role: An Interview Study of Men Who Experience Violence from Female Partners). Master's dissertation, Institutt for sosiologi og samfunnsgeografi (The Department of Sociology and Human Geography), University of Oslo. Retrieved from https://www.duo.uio.no/handle/10852/15305.

Corbally, M. (2015). Accounting for Intimate Partner Violence. *Journal of Interpersonal Violence, 30*(17), 3112–3132.

David, D. S., & Brannon, R. (1976). *The Forty-Nine Percent Majority: The Male Sex Role*. Reading, MA: Addison-Wesley.

Fjell, T. (2013). *Den usynliggjorte volden: Om menn som utsettes for partnervold fra kvinner (The Invisible Violence: About Men Subjected to Partner Violence from Women)*. Trondheim: Akademika forlag.

Gottzén, L. (2016). Displaying Shame: Men's Violence Towards Women in a Culture of Gender Equality. In *Response Based Approaches to the Study of Interpersonal Violence* (pp. 156–175). London: Palgrave Macmillan.

Grøvdal, Y., Jonassen, W., & Nasjonalt kunnskapssenter om vold og traumatisk stress. (2015). *Menn på krisesenter (Men at Crisis Centres)* (Vol. 5/2015), Report (Nasjonalt kunnskapssenter om vold og traumatisk stress: published version) (The Norwegian Centre for Violence and Traumatic Stress Studies). Oslo: Nasjonalt kunnskapssenter om vold og traumatisk stress (The Norwegian Centre for Violence and Traumatic Stress Studies). Retrieved from https://www.nkvts.no/rapport/menn-pa-krisesenter/.

Haaland, T., Clausen, S., & Schei, B. (2005). *Vold i parforhold—ulike perspektiver: Resultater fra den første landsdekkende undersøkelsen i Norge* [Violence in Partner Relationships—Various Perspectives: Results from the First Nationwide Survey in Norway] (Vol. 2005:3, NIBR-rapport). Oslo: Norsk institutt for by- og regionforskning (Norwegian Institute for Urban and Regional Research). Retrieved from http://www.hioa.no/Om-HiOA/Senter-for-velferds-og-arbeidslivsforskning/NIBR/Publikasjoner/Publikasjoner-norsk/Vold-i-parforhold-ulike-perspektiver.

Johnson, M. (2008). *A Typology of Domestic Violence: Intimate Terrorism, Violent Resistance, and Situational Couple Violence.* Boston: Northeastern University Press.

Kimmel, M. (2002). "Gender Symmetry" in Domestic Violence. *Violence Against Women, 8*(11), 1332–1363.

Pape, H., & Stefansen, K. (2004). *Den Skjulte volden?: En undersøkelse av Oslobefolkningens utsatthet for trusler, vold og seksuelle overgrep* [The Hidden Violence?: A Study of the Vulnerability to Threats, Violence and Sexual Assault of Oslo's Population] (Vol. Nr 1/2004, Rapport (Nasjonalt kunnskapssenter om vold og traumatisk stress: online)). Nasjonalt kunnskapssenter om vold og traumatisk stress (The Norwegian Centre for Violence and Traumatic Stress Studies). Retrieved from https://www.nkvts.no/rapport/den-skjulte-volden-en-undersokelse-av-oslobefolkningens-utsatthet-for-trusler-vold-og-seksuelle-overgrep/.

Seidler, V. (1997). *Man Enough: Embodying Masculinities.* London: Sage.

Simmons, J., Wijma, B., & Swahnberg, K. (2014). Associations and Experiences Observed for Family and Nonfamily Forms of Violent Behaviour in Different Relational Contexts Among Swedish Men and Women. *Violence and Victims, 29*(1), 152–170.

Thoresen, S., & Hjemdal, O. K. (2014). *Vold og voldtekt i Norge: En nasjonal forekomststudie av vold i et livsløpsperspektiv (Violence and Rape in Norway: A national prevalence study of violence in a lifespan perspective)* (Vol. 1/2014), Report (Nasjonalt kunnskapssenter om vold og traumatisk stress: trykt utg) (The Norwegian Centre for Violence and Traumatic Stress Studies). Oslo: Nasjonalt kunnskapssenter om vold og traumatisk stress (The Norwegian Centre for Violence and Traumatic Stress Studies). Retrieved from https://www.nkvts.no/rapport/vold-og-voldtekt-i-norge-en-nasjonal-forekomst-studie-av-vold-i-et-livslopsperspektiv/.

Open Access This chapter is licensed under the terms of the Creative Commons Attribution 4.0 International License (http://creativecommons.org/licenses/by/4.0/), which permits use, sharing, adaptation, distribution and reproduction in any medium or format, as long as you give appropriate credit to the original author(s) and the source, provide a link to the Creative Commons licence and indicate if changes were made.

The images or other third party material in this chapter are included in the chapter's Creative Commons licence, unless indicated otherwise in a credit line to the material. If material is not included in the chapter's Creative Commons licence and your intended use is not permitted by statutory regulation or exceeds the permitted use, you will need to obtain permission directly from the copyright holder.

5

Consequences of Intimate Partner Violence

Although the men in our study have experienced frequent physical and psychological attacks, the physical violence has not necessarily been life threatening. The men have suffered both minor and more serious physical injuries. Blisters, minor cuts, bruised eyes, groin pain, bites, scratched hands and backs are the most common physical injuries reported. One man suffered severe concussion and cuts after his wife attacked him and pushed him over.

Most of the men have suffered a variety of psychological problems both during and after the relationship, such as insomnia, difficulties in concentration, and a deep sense of insecurity and unease. Some struggle with trauma and social anxiety.

The men who experienced a pattern of violence over a longer period of time describe more serious health complaints than those who got out of the relationship relatively early on. Five men said they had gone so low psychologically that they played with the idea of ending their own lives. Three actually attempted suicide.

© The Author(s) 2019
M. I. Lien, J. Lorentzen, *Men's Experiences of Violence in Intimate Relationships*,
Palgrave Studies in Victims and Victimology,
https://doi.org/10.1007/978-3-030-03994-3_5

Exhaustion, Anxiety and Depression

Fredrik, Harald and Jon all suffered with anxiety for several years after the end of their relationships. Harald has been in psychotherapy for several years after his divorce. He describes periods after the breakup during which he felt anger and despair at having so many years of his life wrecked, because of his wife's violence and anger: he still experiences panic, anxiety and fear in situations that are very ordinary and present no actual danger. For example, he can feel the urge to flee when his present wife tickles him or touches him with long nails. It reminds him of his ex-wife scratching his face, his back and his hands so hard that she drew blood.

Andreas went into depression when his son was 2.5 years old and received psychological help to cope with the contact time with his son. He was completely exhausted after visiting his son and ex-girlfriend, and nearly collapsed because he had used up all his energy on satisfying an unstable ex-cohabitant's controlling and harassing behaviour.

More than half of the men felt lonely because they had isolated themselves and lost contact with their friends and networks. This isolation was a consequence of a sense of being excluded and anxiety about being a bad person.

Fredrik's wife used the abuse he had experienced as a boy against him. Harassing him sexually and humiliating him, she tore down his identity and his feelings of self-worth. She continually pointed out how unattractive he was to anyone but her. When the child custody case between Fredrik and his ex-wife escalated, he slumped into a depression, ending up in hospital. He could not take any more and wanted to end his life.

Several men say they have had to build themselves up again after getting out of their relationships. Filip says that even three years after the breakup he still suffers from anxiety in many situations. He often feels that people with whom he is close might be judging him negatively: "It's like I never know if anyone really likes me." Harald has been diagnosed with post-traumatic stress disorder (PTSD) as a result of the violence to which he was subjected and he has applied for criminal injuries compensation. He says that without the long-term therapy he has received and his new girlfriend, he would never have managed to get where he is today. New marriages and/or psychological support have also helped Fredrik, Andreas, Tom and Jon to improve their lives after the breakup of their violent relationships. Filip battled with insomnia and difficulties with concentration, eventually losing his job as a driver after he fell asleep at the wheel. He was on sick leave for one year due to anxiety and depression and had to change his line of work in order to get back into employment. For Albert, the conflict over access had no consequences on his work situation, but it absorbed time and energy and reduced his quality of life for long periods of time. Jonas says "I try not to have personal relationships, I try not to get involved in other people's lives" and he feels that he almost erased himself. Meanwhile, Peter says that he "avoids all confrontation", Deo has felt extremely lonely, and Arild says that he was cowed in the relationship; several men either feared for their lives or wanted to die.

Andreas's financial situation deteriorated badly after he went through the courts about his contact rights. He did not have the resources to hire a lawyer to continue the case further in the judicial system. Tor went to court several times about contact, but lost. He found, as did other men in the sample, that he was not believed or seen as able to care adequately for his child. When he first met his ex-wife he had a good job and a good income and well-ordered finances. After a tumultuous conflict and court case, which resulted in his wife being awarded full parental control, he had a breakdown, lost control at work and went onto disability benefits. He says that his life was destroyed after he lost contact with his daughter.

Increased Use of Alcohol

Half of the men say they have used alcohol to escape their everyday lives and the stresses of the situation. Andreas said that if he had not met his current wife, he might easily have gone into depression and turned to alcohol to stay afloat. Harald first started drinking after his ex-wife died one year after the breakup. He drank to feel better and after three glasses of wine he felt "almost" normal. He would sit and drink after the children had gone to bed.

Jon started drinking a lot after his relationship ended. He sat alone and drank and did not seek any help to deal with his feelings. A friend almost forced him to seek help at the local psychiatric unit (DPS), where he has had treatment for several years.

Christian does not suffer any long-term effects from his turbulent marriage, but when the conflicts and sense of unrest were at their worst, he dealt with his feelings by drinking more than usual. He drank to escape everyday life and so he could sleep. Christian's drinking habits led to him taking an increased number of days off work with hangovers and anxiety.

Consequences Particular to Immigrant Men

For some of the men, violence has had such a significant effect on their quality of life that much of the interview is taken up with this subject. Since we consciously recruited several men from minority groups, it was interesting to see if they would display any differences to the ethnic Norwegian men. The findings here are quite clear: the consequences of violence in everyday life are more extensive for those foreign men who do not have a permanent right of residence in Norway. The Norwegian men have feared for their lives and suffered a lowering of their living standards, but immigrant men suffer the additional fears of being thrown out of the country and the consequences of that, of being isolated from their own group, and of stigmatisation and loneliness.

From an intersectionality perspective, we see that the combination of several oppression mechanisms gives a more complex picture. Men from minority groups who are exposed to violence in intimate relationships describe a significant reduction in quality of life and enormous loneliness. Two of the men experience the fact that they are gay as an added strain.

Bashir is fighting a battle on several fronts. Almost wherever he goes he is pursued by men from his own region, threatening and bullying him. He sits at home for much of the time, terrified that somebody might come. The only place he feels safe is in the college classroom. Even the college is not completely safe, as in the hallways and at break times he is afraid of other students. Bashir was threatened in his homeland because he was gay and the threats continue in Norway.

I'm sad and afraid, and I'm tired because I've experienced so much in my life. I'm afraid at college and in the corridor. Everyone from my country seems to know me, even though I don't know them, they say "he's gay, he's gay." They say he's a Muslim how can he be gay, I'm going to kill him, they say. They won't do it here [in Norway], I know that, but I'm scared and sad. I don't like being gay, but it is not something I can choose.

Researcher: Are you worried that someone might come and get you?

I feel safe, but my body has had so many problems, so many people have bullied me and said they're going to fuck me and that I'll go to hell. You can't meet God, you'll go to hell. I'm so scared, I was born gay, I'm a failure, I have problems with many things.

Researcher: Do you dream …?

Yes.

Researcher: What do you dream about?

I dream about abuse and that people are bullying me, yelling at me.

Bashir lives with a deep sense of insecurity and even his dreams are nightmares filled with atrocities and abuse. He can never relax completely. An insecure childhood of abuse and violence has left its mark and he shows clear signs of anxiety when we talk to him. The interview with Bashir is also the most difficult we carry out, because at the age of 20 he is marked by such a deep sense of loss and because it is so difficult for him to find any solid foothold in his life.

Researcher: How do you imagine your life in the future?

I hate my life, but I live here and I'm gay. The question is this—I know I live in Norway and I'll have freedom, but because the others bully me I have a broken heart, I have problems here and I can't … some people say I'm going to hell and that's sad, I've thought I'm between life and death. I like my life too. I have problems but I love my life.

What Bashir experienced in childhood was a deep trauma which effected his entire upbringing. Bashar could equally well have been included in the sample of men we will look at in Chap. 6 who are victims of sexual abuse and incest. For this group of men, and for Bashir, we find a different form of traumatisation than among the other men. Problems such as anxiety, guilt, shame, difficulties with social relationships, low self-esteem, and sometimes obsessive compulsive disorder, are prevalent in these men. We will return to this in Chap. 6.

Zaid, 29, was also attacked because he is gay, as well as being forced to flee unrest in his home country. He was persecuted and subject to violence because of his sexual orientation. In Norway, Zaid had a boyfriend who subjected him to serious physical violence on several occasions. After living at the crisis centre for a while, he has since been transferred to NAV (Norwegian Labour and Welfare Administration), who were supposed help him to find a place to live. When we meet Zaid, NAV have still not found him suitable accommodation, and he is forced to move from hotel to hotel. The interview was conducted with an interpreter.

> Researcher: I want to ask you now what you think about your current situation?
> *Very bad. He says [Zaid] that even when he lived in his homeland it was a much, much, much better life than he has here in every way. He says he did not come to Norway to eat, drink and stay in a hotel. I wanted to come here and be a part of society, to give something back to society and contribute to the functioning of society, not sit in a hotel and wait, he says.*

Several times in the interview, he says he hates everything. He came to a peaceful country with respect for gays, found an apartment and moved in with his boyfriend. But now, as a result of the violence, he finds that he is left sitting there with nothing.

For immigrants, the experience of isolation and loneliness can be particularly overwhelming, since their networks are, in the main, made up of married couples.

This was the case for Deo. Deo came to Norway to get married. When he first arrived he was virtually alone in a new milieu, where his wife was not only surrounded by her own family but the complete network of contacts. When Deo decided to leave her because of her violence and threats, he also left behind all the contacts whom he had known since arriving in Norway many years before. His wife's family instructed everyone in the community to have nothing more to do with him.

I cry because I'm very lonely. I come to Norway and have no friends and only have her and her family. I do not have anything else. I cry and I have no one to talk to. The others do not want to talk to me.

Deo cries several times during the interview. Even though he has moved out and the violence has ceased, he is still being contacted by an ex-wife who threatens him. What he finds even worse is that his wife's friends and family members have started to threaten his family back in his homeland, telling them that they are going to kill Deo, and also threatening Deo himself with killing his sister.

For Deo, the help and support he has received at the crisis centre have been crucial for both his understanding of the situation and his ability to go on with his life despite what he has suffered.

As previously mentioned, we consciously recruited men of various ethnicities for this study. Men from immigrant backgrounds are also subjected to violence from both male and female partners, but several of the interviews show that there are often additional complexities to their situation that bring a unique set of fears of what might happen to them. Many find that their residence in Norway is threatened, and without a permanent residence permit they are afraid they might be returned to their country of origin if they move out of the family home—that is, if they leave the violent relationship. They also report being excluded and, in part, bullied by people from their region or country of origin. This applies to both heterosexual and gay men. Men from ethnic backgrounds are thus more prone to marginalisation and exclusion, and will therefore require additional attention from support agencies. It is crucial that these organisations be aware of how the transnational nature of these relationships, and the risk of shaming within the wider family in these men's countries of origin, may lead to additional pressures, and may be an important contributing factor in the failure of minority men to seek help or talk about their experiences of violence.

The challenges related to the threat to rights of residence and the potential for exclusion are the same for female users of crisis centres from a minority background in Norway.

The Importance of Therapy in Identifying Violence

We find that violence affects vulnerable men in various ways, and often to a greater degree than they themselves realise while it is happening. As we have seen, there is a tendency for men to under-communicate the violence they have been subject to, in particular physical violence, and to under-communicate their fear of what could happen—both to themselves and to the children. We find that those men who look back on their experiences, where it has been three or more years since they lived with their violent partner, have both a greater insight into the situation and the concepts to talk about what they have been through.

In our opinion, this has to be seen in light of the fact that these men have been in therapy, or have had someone to talk to who has helped them to process and put words to their experience. As Andreas explained: "It's only in recent years that I've understood that I have been subjected to psychological violence." He points to his new wife and his supportive network of friends as having been decisive in his recovery from years of oppression and sabotage of access.

In most cases we see that the experience of violence has had a fundamental effect on these men. They report that they wanted to present an image of being in control of their lives, while in reality they were isolating themselves increasingly from the outside world and felt more lonely than before. For some of them the physical violence eventually became life threatening. Many of those interviewed expressed that it had been good to talk to us about their experiences. For some, it was the first time they had told their stories to anyone.

It is well documented that violence and sexual abuse in childhood and adulthood have a major impact on mental health later in life (Krug 2002; Finkelhor and Delworth 1990; Walker 1984). In general, such conclusions are based on research on women who have been subjected to violence in intimate relationships. Both physical and psychological partner violence are associated with significant physical and mental health consequences for both female and male victims (Coker et al. 2002; Krug 2002). As we have seen, violence affects men's everyday lives and relationships in many ways. The national surveys *Vold i forhold (Violence in Relationships;* Haaland et al. 2005) and *Vold og voldtekt i Norge (Violence and Rape in Norway;* Thoresen and Hjemdal 2014) also found that violence in intimate relationships has extensive consequences on health. Data from the National Violence Against Women Survey (NVAWS) also showed that physical partner violence is associated with an increased risk of poor physical health, symptoms of depression and increased drug use in both men and women (Coker et al. 2002).

Previous prevalence studies have shown that men exposed to intimate partner violence with use of controlling behaviours are at an increased risk of developing PTSD (Hines and Douglas 2011). Here we wish to point out that both prevalence studies and clinical trials have shown an increased risk of PTSD in both women and men who experience severe partner violence (defined in this study as intimate terrorism). Hines and Douglas's study (2011) also compared the health of men exposed to intimate terrorism to those who have not been exposed to intimate partner violence, and found that there was a higher incidence of PTSD among men who had experienced intimate terrorism than among other men. Allen-Collinson (2009) and Migliaccio (2002) found that men who were victims of partner violence suffered from suicidal thoughts, disassociation and avoidance.

Violence Affects the Children

It is important to emphasise that partner violence is not only destructive and difficult to cope with for the adults involved, but also for the children. As we have seen, in several of the relationships into which we have gained insight over the longer term, the conflict between partners has ended in a breakup, with serious disagreements over the division of parental care of the children. Threats of sabotage of contact, accusations of being a bad father, humiliation and hitting a partner in front of the children are all forms of psychological and physical violence that also have consequences for any children involved. These children have been witness to conflicts, violence and severe disturbance in the family home. Fear, guilt and a feeling of helplessness are frequent reactions to the witnessing of violence between parents. We know from previous studies that to witness conflicts and violence between parents can be as harmful as being the victim of violence oneself (see Mullender et al. 2002; Holt 2008; Mossinge and Stefansen 2016). Children want to be loyal to both parents and often hide any violence in the family. All the fathers in this sub-study describe situations in which their children have needed intervention from the school health services, BUP (Norway's Children's and Young People's Psychiatric Services) or other health services. There has also been shown to be a strong correlation in Norwegian studies between being a witness to violence and becoming a victim (Mossinge and Stefansen 2016). Again, this knowledge is largely based on families where fathers are the perpetrators. Since there are few studies of male victims' qualitative experiences of violence in intimate relationships, we also lack knowledge of how children are affected by the violence of mothers against fathers. Based on previous research, however, it is reasonable to assume that the consequences on the children are serious—irrespective of which partner is the perpetrator.

Lack of Self-Worth

We have described how men experience problems of diminished self-esteem and social anxiety as a result of living for many years with ridicule, silence, rejection and humiliation. Some felt that their confidence had been so worn down by their partner that they had lost their grip on life entirely. One man described ending up in the accident and emergency department after collapsing in the street with an epileptic fit. When he got back home and told his partner, she acted as though he was not even in the room.

Jon is the only man in this sub-study who was already depressed before he met his partner. As mentioned earlier in this chapter, his early years were marked by insecurity and bullying at school. His reaction to this violence was to take an "underdog position" to avoid further problems. The vulnerability he brought with him into this relationship is probably a key reason for his non-retaliation and for his staying in the relationship so long. In addition, the father of his partner had acted as guarantor for the loan for their apartment, making him financially dependent on her.

As seen previously, men have a tendency not to recognise that they have been subjected to serious violence until after the breakup, and/or they trivialise the violence and believe they ought to be able to deal with it. Those who were, or had been, in their relationships for a long time did not talk to others about the violence while they were still in the relationship. In line with other studies, we found that talking to others about the violence, and in particular seeking assistance from relevant organisations, is central to men's ability to make the decision and carry through the breakup of such relationships (Haaland et al. 2005, p. 151).

Psychological Violence

At the beginning of Chap. 4, we described some of the men's childhood experiences of violence. Some had particularly difficult experiences with peers and/or describe themselves as insecure children. We will now look at how Fredrik and Harald reflect on their vulnerability in relation to the partner violence to which they were later subjected.

Fredrik says that as an adult he has lived with a great deal of uncertainty and fear because of the abuse he experienced as a child. He believes that his fear of being inadequate and the damage he suffered from this earlier abuse contributed to his taking a subordinate role in his marriage. He lived for over ten years with a wife who subjected both himself and their two children to serious physical and psychological violence. According to Fredrik, his past experiences of abuse became an effective tool for his wife to use in controlling and suppressing him. He was afraid to leave his wife, because he had internalised the idea that nobody else would want to be with such a bad person and partner as he was. In addition, he had a stepdaughter and two children whom he did not want to hurt or make problems for.

Harald tried several times during the interview to explain why he had ended up in such a chaotic relationship when he had been so withdrawn and careful as a youngster. He thinks he stayed because he wanted to help his wife and stabilise the everyday lives of the two children. Since their mother was so unstable, he needed to compensate and offer them security.

As we have mentioned, there are several men in our material who have considered or attempted suicide. Some find it difficult to get involved with other people even years after the relationship has ended. We see many similarities between men's experiences and what previous studies show about women's experiences with partner violence. In the Norwegian book about domestic violence against women and children *Bjørnen sover (The Bear Sleeps)*, Alsaker writes about how offensive and insulting behaviour and the abuse of trust destroy women's trust in both themselves and others (Storberget et al. 2007). Insults can, in the contexts of a love or care relationship, be especially difficult to cope with, and the men in our study have gone to great lengths to avoid causing irritation or conflict with their partners by doing what they think is expected of them. Similar avoidance strategies are also found in studies of women living in abusive relationships (Walker 1984; Follingstad et al. 2002; Storberget et al. 2007). In her book *The Battered Woman*, the American psychologist Lenore Walker (1984) describes how psychological degradation, fear and humiliation were the forms of abuse which women found most painful. On the basis of previous studies of women who suffer male partner violence, Walker assumed that women would say that threats of physical violence and destruction of property were the forms of psychological violence which they most feared from their partners. However, the study showed that women's fear of humiliation and ridicule impacted them most (Walker 1984, p. 117). Feelings of guilt, self-reproach and the fear of not being a good enough husband and father are additional important driving factors for men staying in violent relationships. Some have been so isolated that for long periods they have been without any networks or any friends to whom they could talk. The majority of men say that they have, or have had, social anxiety and felt completely worthless while they were living in the relationship. As we have described, several of the men have experienced threats to being deprived of access to the children, and fear of destroying the family has contributed to their failure to report violence.

Why Do Men Stay in Violent Relationships?

We find a varied picture of the reasons why men stay in violent relationships. Those men who have stayed in their relationships for a long time have all taken an actively caring role towards their children and had a desire to help their wives and girlfriends who struggled in the workplace, or had difficulties or psychological problems. A desire to protect the children and the wider family from a family breakup also acts as an important driving force for men to remain, despite any conflict and violence. Several men said they had spent a lot of time trying to find explanations for the violence, why they had been subjected to it and why had they stayed for so long. Phrases like "surreal", "removed from reality", "living in a bubble" and "madness" were used for the relationship they had found themselves in. Several had asked themselves: How in the world did I get into this situation? Why did this happen to *me*? and Why didn't I set boundaries earlier?

Summary of Findings

The majority of the men in our sample have been subjected to various forms of partner violence. Most have been subjected to severe and systematic violence over several years. The stories told by several of those men who did not seek the help of crisis centres indicate that they might well have needed overnight accommodation and the chance to talk for shorter or longer periods. Only 1 per cent of residents in crisis centres in Norway are referred by the family protection service (Bufdir 2016, p. 13). This low referral rate may indicate that the family protection service has little skill in detecting ongoing partner violence between spouses or partners.

We have also found a distinctive form of violence to which men are subjected, namely what we have termed the "switching of the violence relationship". It is a significant problem for men that their violent female partners are in a position to turn reality on its head and tell everyone that *they* are the victims of violence. This is because the accepted social discourse makes it easy for women to be believed when it comes to their being the victims of violence in intimate relationships, while men are generally not believed. In such cases this makes the men feel doubly helpless. They themselves internalise this understanding, and feel that nothing can help them, because "no one will believe me anyway".

Another interesting finding is that despite the violence they are subjected to, these men express a great deal of care and love for their wives/girlfriends/boyfriends, and try to understand and protect them. They are reluctant, for example, to report the violence to the police for the sake of their partners. This caring attitude makes it more difficult for men to seek help and look after themselves. They put their own needs aside, and state very clearly when questioned that they thought they could handle the violence to which they were being subjected until it became very serious or dangerous. The men we interviewed also talk about children who have been present during incidents of family violence and conflicts. As discussed previously, children suffer both short-term and long-term damage as a result of witnessing conflicts and violence between their parents. The men who have lived in violent relationships with women for a long time say that their partners have dominated them psychologically through a variety of different types of controlling behaviour. Several of the men have been threatened with being deprived of contact with the children, and say that the fear of destroying their families has contributed to their failure to report the violence.

Our study shows that self-reproach, shame of being a victim of violence and social anxiety seem to be universal, rather than gendered, phenomena among people who experience violence from those who are close to them. Those men who have lived in violent relationships have taken time to recognise and process the violence to which they have been subjected.

The men we interviewed trivialised the violence to themselves and others for a long time. Some of the respondents from the crisis centres, and most of the men from immigrant backgrounds, had difficulty using the term "violence", even where severe physical violence had been used. When they have been in contact with support agencies, these men have often failed to mention the violence. They perceived that they did not fit into the organisation's image of victim and perpetrator, and have been frightened of not being believed, because the violence to which they have been subjected does not conform to any stereotype. This is important to understand if we are to reach men who struggle with violent experiences and who need help to get out of such relationships and process their feelings.

We have taken our starting point in the experiences of these men of partner violence, and have no insight into the lives of their partners (either female or male) apart from the accounts given by interviewees. As previously mentioned, those men who have experienced systematic and severe violence over time have been involved with women (and men) with psychological problems, who appear to lack adequate coping strategies to deal with conflict.

Based on the men's stories of violence from their partners (both male and female), it is pertinent to ask whether mental illnesses can explain a significant proportion of the causes of the violence to which the men in this study have been subjected. In future research on violence against men, it will be important to investigate the root cause(s) of this violence.

As mentioned earlier, we find an interesting ambivalence in men's attitudes between traditional ideals of masculinity as protectors and providers, and their experiences as victims of violence. How men negotiate the idea of the male provider and their own desire to/expectation that they should protect their wives and children, with their understanding of themselves as the victim of violence, is a topic that has received little attention thus far in violence research. We have merely touched on this subject in this book, and see the need for further studies in this area.

Interviews with those men who have experienced intimate partner violence and then sought help at crisis centres show that men are also subjected to systematic and, in part, serious physical abuse, despite the fact that it seems that psychological violence is the most widespread and profound in these men's stories. They are subjected to violence from both male and female partners, but sexual orientation has little to do with the experience of violence. The traumatising effect that violence has on the individual is very similar, regardless of the kind of relationship the victim is living in.

However, there is one significant difference between the vulnerability of gay men versus heterosexual men in this sample, and that is the experience of sexual violence. Two of the men with gay partners have been subjected to systematic sexual assault and rape, while only one of the heterosexual men describes verbal sexual insults. This is in line with prevalence studies that show that male victims of female perpetrators rarely experience severe sexual violence. Our material is of course extremely limited, but these gay men's experiences of coercion and sexual abuse may help contextualise and illustrate how sexual violence in gay relationships takes place. The violence to which gay men are subjected may therefore have a more complex profile.

Discussion

In the 1970s, there was a sea change in the understanding of domestic violence, from being one where violence in intimate relationships was regarded as a uniquely personal problem for women caused by individual men's psychological problems, to one where the abuse of women or marital violence was regarded as a wider social problem resulting from overarching patriarchal power structures (Lawson 2012, p. 573). Research into women contributed greatly to putting women's experiences of violence and oppression in intimate relationships on the agenda in the fields of research, politics and the general public discourse about family violence. This resulted in the establishment of an ideological debate about masculinity, violence and suppression of women, which further influenced politics and resulted in the establishment of various programmes and support agencies for women and children subjected to violence (see Tjaden and Thoennes 2000).

Violence in intimate relationships was a central theme in the struggle for equality by political agencies. Today, the focus has to some degree changed in Norway, in that gender equality policy now looks at men's experiences and living conditions too. However, the established ideological gender violence discourse can be regarded as a meta-discourse that puts a strong emphasis on our understanding of the victims and perpetrators of violence. Research into men's experiences of partner violence reveals stories that challenge established discourses. Such institutionalised discourses can play an important mediating role in that they become sources and resources that staff in support organisations draw upon, consciously or unconsciously, in their encounters with men and women in relationships characterised by conflict. There is reason to believe that a gender bias exists within the support system as a result of the traditional gender-power perspective still being the dominant one, and that this perspective helps to define what men (and women) can say or do in their encounters with support agencies (Smith 2006, p. 34).

The established gender-power discourse on women's abuse still exists within the support agencies, in the public arena and, as we have seen, the minds of those men who are subjected to physical and psychological abuse by women and other men. In several of the men's stories we find a mindset that says "I am not a real victim" or "I ought to be able to bear this because I am a man".

Despite the many positive experiences with support agencies, it is clear that there are still enormous challenges ahead in reaching out to men with the help they need. In a Norwegian context, we have come a long way as regards gender equality and in highlighting and recognising that men can be victims of intimate partner violence. It is now established in Norwegian law that a proportion of these men need longer-term help from support agencies and, in certain cases, protection (Lov om kommunale krisesentertilbud/Law on the availability of council crisis centres). Norway's Children Youth and Family Directorate stipulates clearly that violence in intimate relationships also affects men and that support agencies must work to improve resources for male victims of violence.

De Welde (2003) claims that "hegemonic discourses of women's powerlessness are not equipped to deal with power from women" (p. 250). Bringing greater nuance to and establishing parallel discourses and theories about the workings of power and partner violence must not be seen as a subordination or rejection of our understanding that violence against women is a major societal problem that requires significant intervention both locally, nationally and globally.

References

Allen-Collinson, J. (2009). A Marked Man: Female-Perpetrated Intimate Partner Abuse. *International Journal of Men's Health, 8*(1), 22–40.

Barne-, ungdoms- og familiedirektoratet (Bufdir). (2016). Rapportering fra krisesentertilbudene 2015. (Norwegian Child, Youth and Family Directorate (Bufdir). Report of Services Offered by Crisis Centres 2015) Report 11/2016. Retrieved from https://www.bufdir.no/global/Rapportering_fra_krisesentertilbudene_2015.pdf.

Coker, A. L., Davis, K. E., Arias, I., Desai, S., Sanderson, M., Brandt, H. M., & Smith, P. H. (2002). Physical and Mental Health Effects of Intimate Partner Violence for Men and Women. *American Journal of Preventive Medicine, 23*(4), 260–268.

De Welde, K. (2003). Getting Physical: Subverting Gender Through Selfdefense. *Journal of Contemporary Ethnography, 32*(3), 247–278.

Finkelhor, D., & Delworth, U. (1990). Early and Long-Term Effects of Child Sexual Abuse: An Update. *Professional Psychology: Research and Practice, 21*(5), 325–330.

Follingstad, D. R., Bradley, R. G., Helff, C. M., & Laughlin, J. E. (2002). A Model for Predicting Dating Violence: Anxious Attachment, Angry Temperament and a Need for Relationship Control. *Violence and Victims, 17*, 35–47.

Haaland, T., Clausen, S., & Schei, B. (2005). *Vold i parforhold—ulike perspektiver: Resultater fra den første landsdekkende undersøkelsen i Norge (Violence in Partner Relationships—Various Perspectives: Results from the First Nationwide Survey in Norway)* (Vol. 2005:3, NIBR-report). Oslo: Norsk institutt for by- og regionforskning (Norwegian Institute for Urban and Regional Research). Retrieved from http://www.hioa.no/Om-HiOA/Senter-for-velferds-og-arbeidslivsforskning/NIBR/Publikasjoner/Publikasjoner-norsk/Vold-i-parforhold-ulike-perspektiver.

Hines, D. A., & Douglas, E. M. (2011). Symptoms of Post Traumatic Stress Disorder in Men Who Sustain Intimate Partner Violence: A Study of Helpseeking and Community Samples. *Psychology of Men & Masculinity, 12*(2), 112–127.

Holt, S. (2008). The Impact of Exposure to Domestic Violence on Children and Young People: A Review of the Literature. *Child Abuse & Neglect: The International Journal, 32*(8), 797–810.

Krug, E. (2002). *World Report on Violence and Health.* Geneva: World Health Organization. Retrieved from http://www.who.int/violence_injury_prevention/violence/world_report/en/.

Lawson, J. (2012). Sociological Theories of Intimate Partner Violence. *Journal of Human Behavior in the Social Environment, 22*(5), 572–590.

Migliaccio, T. (2002). Abused Husbands. *Journal of Family Issues, 23*(1), 26–52.

Mossinge, S., & Stefansen, K. (2016). *Vold og overgrep mot barn og unge. Omfang og utviklingstrekk 2007–2015* [Violence and Abuse Against Children and Adolescents in Norway: Prevalence and Development from 2007–2015]. NOVA report. OsloMet University. Retrieved from http://www.hioa.no/content/download/125214/3227117/file/Vold-og-overgrep-mot-barn-og-ung-NOVA-Rapport-5-16-web.pdf.

Mullender, A., Hague, G., Imam, U., Kelly, L., Malos, E., & Regan, L. (2002). *Children's Perspectives on Domestic Violence.* London: SAGE Publications.

Smith, D. E. (2006). *Institutional Ethnography as Practice.* Lanham, MD: Rowman & Littlefield.

Storberget, K., Bråten, B., Rømming, E., Skjørten, K., & Aas-Hansen, A. (Red.) (2007). *Bjørnen sover. Om vold i familien (The Bear Sleeps. About Violence in the Family).* Oslo: Aschehoug & Co.

Thoresen, S., & Hjemdal, O. K. (2014). *Vold og voldtekt i Norge: En nasjonal forekomststudie av vold i et livsløpsperspektiv (Violence and Rape in Norway: A National Prevalence Study of Violence in a Lifespan Perspective)* (Vol. 1/2014), Rapport (Nasjonalt kunnskapssenter om vold og traumatisk stress: published version.) (The Norwegian Centre for Violence and Traumatic Stress Studies). Oslo: Nasjonalt kunnskapssenter om vold og traumatisk stress (The Norwegian Centre for Violence and Traumatic Stress Studies). Retrieved from https://www.nkvts.no/rapport/vold-og-voldtekt-i-norge-en-nasjonal-forekomststudie-av-vold-i-et-livslopsperspektiv/.

Tjaden, P., Thoennes, N., Centers for Disease Control Prevention, & National Institute of Justice. (2000). *Full Report of the Prevalence, Incidence, and Consequences of Violence Against Women: Findings from the National Violence Against Women Survey.* U.S. Department of Justice, Office of Justice Programs, National Institute of Justice.

Walker, L. (1984). *The Battered Woman Syndrome* (Vol. 6, Springer series, Focus on Women). New York: Springer.

Open Access This chapter is licensed under the terms of the Creative Commons Attribution 4.0 International License (http://creativecommons.org/licenses/by/4.0/), which permits use, sharing, adaptation, distribution and reproduction in any medium or format, as long as you give appropriate credit to the original author(s) and the source, provide a link to the Creative Commons licence and indicate if changes were made.

The images or other third party material in this chapter are included in the chapter's Creative Commons licence, unless indicated otherwise in a credit line to the material. If material is not included in the chapter's Creative Commons licence and your intended use is not permitted by statutory regulation or exceeds the permitted use, you will need to obtain permission directly from the copyright holder.

6

Men Who Are Subjected to Sexual Abuse

Although the following extracts are taken from interviews with men who sought help because they had been subjected to sexual abuse, it should be stressed that no absolute boundaries can be drawn between various forms of violence. Men who appear elsewhere in this study who sought and obtained help at other crisis centres for physical and psychological violence may also have experienced sexual abuse. It is common for men who have been subjected to sexual violence to be subjected to physical violence too. Where interview material showed or indicated psychological violence or neglect of care, this has been noted. A host of studies show that children and young people who are the victim of one traumatic event are often the victim of further similar events, a fact termed poly-victimisation in the research (Finkelhor et al. 2007).

Since research in recent decades has also shown the profound psychological consequences of psychological violence and neglect—that is, not only violence which is manifest physically and can therefore cause physical damage and pain—we have chosen to include evidence of such experiences where they are indicated in our material.

Most of the men interviewed were middle-aged (between 36 and 48 years), with the exception of one younger man (28) and two who were

© The Author(s) 2019
M. I. Lien, J. Lorentzen, *Men's Experiences of Violence in Intimate Relationships*,
Palgrave Studies in Victims and Victimology,
https://doi.org/10.1007/978-3-030-03994-3_6

over 60. Our sample represents a relatively broad spectrum of men who have differing circumstances in life and occupation. Some lived alone, with or without their own children, or were divorced. Others were married or lived with a girlfriend, with or without their own children or stepchildren, or had children who had moved out (and grandchildren).

To What Kind of Abuse Have These Men Been Subjected?

A striking number of the men interviewed here had experiences that dated back to their early teens or pre-dated puberty (10–15 years). In many cases the abuse took place for a limited time at this age; sometimes it continued until much later. But there are some who were subjected to abuse from an even earlier age (4–12 years, 6–8 years). In a couple of cases there are also experiences of recurrent sexual abuse in adulthood, or in one case what may more precisely be described as a form of sexual blackmail which was experienced as offensive and psychologically damaging.

The extent of the abuse suffered varies greatly, from discrete episodes (although sometimes on more than one occasion) to a number of times within a limited time frame, or regularly committed by the same perpetrator over a period of several years. A number of men have also been subjected to abuse a number of times by different perpetrators.

Often, but far from always, interviewees also report other forms of violence during childhood and adolescence. Many have experienced, or witnessed, frightening physical violence, or threats or been subjected to psychological violence, or have experienced neglect. The latter can also be seen as a form of violence from a psycho-developmental and human existential perspective. This definition is incidentally consistent with that used by Sogn and Hjemdal in a previous report on violence against men in intimate relationships (Sogn and Hjemdal 2010).

The perpetrators have generally been family members or otherwise close, but their profile differs widely: in some cases fathers or stepfathers were responsible for the abuse (3), in others an uncle (3), and finally neighbours or acquaintances of one of the parents. The latter category includes a postman and a scout leader. Many, but not all, of the perpetrators are men. In one case the perpetrator is a female friend of the father, in another a slightly older girl. In the case of one of the interviewees, an aunt was in part responsible for the abuse; while not abusing her nephew herself, she contributed indirectly to the creation of an abusive situation. In another case, a mother-in-law subjected her son-in-law to unwanted sexual activity for years. It should also be noted that the mother of one of the interviewees frequently hit him when he was a child. Another mother threatened her son and his brothers with violence from their father in his absence, and supported the physical punishment of the boys in various ways.

Experiences of Violence in Childhood

Sexual Violence

All those whose stories are summarised and analysed here were subjected to sexual violence during childhood and/or adolescence. Here are some of the men's own stories about their concrete experiences.

Bjarnar (48) was 11 years old when he accompanied his father (a construction worker) on a job for a man in the village. At one point Bjarnar was left alone with this man, who then took him into the forest behind the house where he lived. There the 11-year-old was undressed and subjected to oral and anal penetration. The man who abused him said he "was as nice as a little girl". Later this was repeated just over half a dozen times by the same perpetrator, who threatened the boy that if he told someone about what had happened, he would be killed. The use of such threats is found in several of the interviewees' stories, and is one of the explanations of their keeping quiet about their experiences.

Terje (46) was first assaulted sexually at the age of 9, by a neighbour and acquaintance of his mother. Although this only happened a couple of times, and was limited to Terje being forced to touch the man's genitals, it was a terrifying experience for one so young. The perpetrator also had a tendency to be physically violent, as witnessed by Terje in other situations. Later, when he was 12, Terje was again subjected to abuse, this time more persistently and for a longer period of time by another man. This man also lived in the neighbourhood and was also acquainted with Terje's mother. The abuse, often oral, could sometimes be repeated several times on the same day, and lasted over a period of at least six months.

Kjartan (36) used to spend time with his uncle, who worked in a newspaper and sweets kiosk in the evenings. Kjartan's uncle allowed him to have all the sweets he wanted. His uncle was also a taxi driver and used to pick up his nephew in his car. Kjartan sometimes stayed the night at the house of his uncle, who drank heavily and watched pornographic films. It was on these nights that the abuse generally took place, although it sometimes happened during the day. This abuse started when Kjartan was only 4 or 5 years old and continued until he was 11 or 12, but was at its worst at about the time he started school, aged 7.

This combination of an abundance of sweets, soft drinks or food, offered at a perpetrator's home, while simultaneously watching porn movies, is one that turns up in several of the men's accounts.

In the case of Odd (63), the perpetrator was a former girlfriend of his father. Odd's mother had died when he was 10 years old and he grew up alone with his father. However, the father was unable to care properly for his son; indeed, he was unable to really take care of himself. He had many, more or less temporary, relationships with various women. When his father was no longer interested in a certain "friend", her focus shifted onto Odd instead. She made him food and bathed him, something nobody else was doing. Bathing Odd gradually evolved into a form of sexual foreplay. As part of the child's bath-time ritual, she masturbated him "and used me in bed and … I did things with her like, yes, did what you do, yes, I was told to do things and I did them …". This lasted for several years until Odd put a stop to the abuse himself.

Range of Violence: Corporal Punishment, Bullying and Psychological Violence

A couple, or at most a few, of the men appear to have grown up in relatively stable and secure environments. Nonetheless, there are sometimes signs that might suggest things were not quite right. Bjarnar grew up in a seemingly safe and normal family, but was exposed to sexual abuse outside the family, and was not listened to by his parents or teachers when he complained about the bullying he was suffering in school. This contributed to Bjarnar keeping quiet about the sexual abuse. Kjartan explains that his parents both had good jobs and have been married for years. In that sense, his family home was stable. Yet both Kjartan and his two brothers have all become drug addicts. Anders (45) describes a secure upbringing in a small community in northern Norway. He experienced no physical or sexual abuse from close family members, but was probably abused by an uncle in another town. At the same time, there are suggestions that strong language was used in the home and that his mother, exhausted and mentally unstable, would shame him and induce guilt in him verbally.

In the majority of the other cases, the circumstances in which these men grew up were more obviously unstable, often with instances of explicit violence.

The wide variety of difficult childhood experiences is illustrated by the account of one of the study's older interviewees, Odd. As a child, he experienced both neglect and sexual abuse. In addition, Odd's time at school was, as he describes it, characterised by "absolutely terrible bullying". His mother died when he was 10 years old and his father could not give the son the care he needed. Nobody bathed Odd or ensured he had proper clothes, or comforted him or made moves to ensure that the bullying he was experiencing in school stopped.

Three participants describe the regular use of corporal punishment during childhood. Sølve (61) was subjected to a form of punishment by his father that crossed the boundary between physical and sexualised violence. When Sølve or one of his brothers had done something to anger their strictly religious and authoritarian parents, they were forced to strip off and go and fetch the stick used to punish them. They then had to go into the bathroom, where whichever boy was being punished had to lie on his father's knee. Before the punishment was executed, it was announced how many strokes had been given on the previous occasion, to which number two additional strokes were added for the punishment that day. Sølve also noticed that his father had an erection when he beat them, and the harder he hit them, the stronger his erection became.

Odd was beaten with a belt by his father. "He hit me … he was a man with hard hitting opinions …,". Ola (46) was also often hit as a small boy, but by his mother. Here, physical punishment seems to have been more impulsive and unpredictable. His mother could hit him without him really understanding the reason for it. In retrospect, he believes that he was simply unable to live up to her expectations of him, either in his behaviour or his aptitude. At the same time, Ola had no real help from her in understanding what was required of him. There was, he says, a lot of screaming and emotional abuse, often under the influence of alcohol, which could without warning also turn into physical abuse. The interviewee describes his mother as a guilt-tripper, erratic and psychologically absent.

Witnessing Violence and Sexual Abuse

Ola also describes his grandfather (on his mother's side) who, although she never actually beat him, was a heavy drinker who liked to fight. Ola's grandfather was a manual worker and extremely strong. The men whom Ola's mother brought home often got a taste of his grandfather's fists. Ola describes his mother as a narcissist: "She was always dragging men back to my grandfather's apartment all the time, and he'd fling them out again, and I watched on. That was my first 12 years of life."

Although Ola describes having positive feelings for his grandfather, these violent episodes had a deep and negative impact on the boy's mind. On one occasion, for example, when he and his grandfather were returning from a food-shopping trip, they got into a heated exchange with some boys in the park. This ended with the grandfather lashing out at them with a bottle of fruit squash. Later, when Ola went to mix himself some squash, he discovered that there was blood on the bottle. When asked how these events affected him, Ola says that he was already dissociating himself from most of his unpleasant experiences; that is, he had developed the tendency to protect himself and shut off his emotional life.

Joar (28) reports that he has been constantly surrounded by conflict and violence since childhood. He saw his mother beaten by his father and witnessed his brother being sexually abused by the father, in addition to suffering abuse himself. Various forms of sexual, physical and psychological violence were a regular part of his everyday life. For example, his father would take his two sons in the car when he was inebriated and drive around at top speed, terrifying them. Despite a relatively early divorce and their relocation, his father repeatedly hunted the family down and continued to terrorise them. Unfortunately, the situation did not improve with either of the two new men with whom his mother went on to have relationships, after divorcing Joar's father and finally managing to escape him. One of the men abused the young boys sexually, while the other was physically and psychologically violent; among other things, Joar was subjected to forced feeding. Their mother was raped within earshot of the children.

Being a witness to violence can be very frightening and have a similar traumatising effect to being exposed to violence oneself, something that is stressed in DSM, the North American psychiatry diagnosis manual. Terje describes a man who was acquainted with his family during his childhood. Although no one in the family was violent themselves, this man was a heavy drinker with a violent temper (he was also sexually abusive towards Terje on a couple of occasions). The violence did not happen in the family home, but when they visited the man's house. Terje describes an incident when this man "got into an argument with some mate of his, who got a thorough beating, got totally smashed up. He was super strong and lifted his mate up and threw him up onto a fence." Naturally, this experience was very frightening for the 9-year-old boy.

Research shows various negative consequences of witnessing violence, as well as a correlation between this phenomenon and other manifestations of violence. Among other things, a clear connection has been documented between the experience of witnessing violence and a vulnerability to violence (Mossige and Stefansen 2016). Children subjected to violence by parents run an increased risk of being subjected to violence by their peers (Mossige and Stefansen 2007). Witnessing and/or suffering violence in the family home has grave consequences on children, since a child's home is the main arena for security and development (Thoresen and Hjemdal 2014; Braarud and Nordanger 2011). WHO reports have also shown a strong link between parents' psychological functioning, stress and family structure, and the risk of child abuse (Krug 2002).

As previously mentioned, the concept of poly-victimisation (Finkelhor et al. 2007) has been used in studies to describe the fact that those who are, for example, subjected to one form of violence very often go on to experience other violence. This is true of most of the men in this study, and we will now look in more detail at these men's experiences of bullying and neglect.

Bullying and Neglect

Like many of the men interviewed, Terje was bullied as a boy: "from the first day of primary school to high school. Almost daily. I had to go the long way to get home because people used to throw stones at me." Odd describes ongoing and painful bullying at school. He turned to his teacher for help, but went unheard. So Odd took the matter in his own hands and armed himself with a bicycle chain. When he was cornered by his classmates one day, he took out the bicycle chain and lashed out with it. His teacher sent him to the head of school and the chain was confiscated. But feeling that he had no one to support him or that he could feel at all safe, Odd now armed himself with a knife, which he hid in his boot.

Erlend (41) describes how his divorced mother met a new man when he was 12 years old, which meant moving to another area. But life was difficult, and he was harassed and bullied. Erlend describes this as a level of humiliation that an adult might handle, but not a child. Among other things, Erlend was forced to act as a chauffeur for his stepfather when he was drunk, despite being no more than 13 years old. After one long evening driving the car (illegally), the boy was too exhausted to go on and his stepfather took over the wheel. Being drunk, he soon drove off the road, but blamed the accident on Erlend.

More than half of the men interviewed describe recurrent bullying in childhood and at school. It would be reasonable to ask if this apparent link between vulnerability to sexual abuse and early bullying is a coincidence, or partly a result of the insecure backgrounds from which most of our participants come. However, since our material is neither extensive enough nor takes this issue as its primary focus, we can only point to the prevalence of childhood bullying in the accounts given in these interviews.

Nevertheless, an indication that such a link may exist appears in research that shows that children with ambivalent attachment issues are frequently impulsive and vulnerable, which in turn often makes them susceptible to bullying (Bunkholdt 2000).

Terje's own reflections on why he was bullied are worth quoting in this context:

> *If you look like a victim, people take you for a victim. If you don't look like a victim you have a better chance of being safe. That experience of bullying at school—they used to hit me. I sat at home and put drawing pins in my clothes so if they hit me they'd get hurt. But whenever I had them on the underside of my arms I never got beat up. Because I wasn't afraid of getting beat up then.*

Clear evidence of childhood neglect emerges in several of the men's accounts, as already discussed, and may be discerned in some of the other interviews. The divorce of parents and abuse of alcohol or drugs all feature regularly in the accounts given by our participants. Several have grown up without a close relationship with a father. A couple of men, on the other hand, have lost their mothers early or lost contact with them. In the vast majority of cases, the siblings of the men interviewed (where there were siblings) have had similar difficult experiences, with similar negative consequences.

Consequences of Sexual and Other Abuse During Childhood

Regardless of how and when the abuse took place, as well as its extent and precise nature, it has had profound and lasting consequences for all the interviewees. Most dramatically, Arne (38) describes the consequences of the abuse he was subjected to as a 12-year-old as a "real before and after". He had a relatively harmonious early childhood, but his parents got divorced when he was 7 years old. It was five years later, when Arne was sexually abused by his football coach, that his life took a dramatic turn: "a few months after that, everything that was good [in my life] caved in. It's clear to see—yes, in my records with doctors and police, and with the drugs and alcohol, and there are several suicide attempts and my admission into a psychiatric [ward] when I was 16." Describing the consequences of abuse in equally dramatic terms, Kjartan says "it destroyed everything in my future. My life, my job, my family, my daughter, everything. My whole life." In Kjartan's case, it appears to have been the resurfacing, five or six years prior to the interview, of partially suppressed memories and emotions connected to the sexual abuse of his childhood which had such a devastating impact on him.

Although there are huge variations in the sorts of psychological impact the abuse had on these men, the kinds of relationship difficulties with which they have since struggled, as well as the extent and duration of their symptoms, the evidence is clear that the effects are pronounced and painful. Symptoms include, for example, intermittent or lasting insomnia, difficulties with concentration and problems with anxiety, in some cases very severe.

Shame and Guilt

Like other children who have been subjected to abuse or violence or other destructive behaviours, the interviewees have also had feelings of shame and guilt about what they experienced. The reaction of shame or the taking on of responsibility for what others have subjected one to may seem strange, but is a very common and widespread phenomenon, especially among children. The logic behind this appears to be that since one is subjected to such appalling and negative experiences, the fault must somehow lie with oneself. This simplistic logic is also often reinforced by the perpetrator or the punishing parent, who will state this to be a fact. For those who have suffered abuse, a sense of shame and guilt seems to be more the rule than the exception.

According to studies by, among others, Mullender et al. (2002) and Steinsvåg (2007), children who grow up with violence in the family experience a sense of disempowerment and feel that the world is fundamentally unpredictable. It is not rare for them to assume responsibility for the violence and to experience guilt because they feel they must have done something wrong to cause it. This affects their self-image and sense of worth, and children with this type of experience often describe a pronounced sense of shame (Mullender et al. 2002; Steinsvåg 2007). This is also evident in our material.

Joar, in particular, feels guilt on behalf of his mother and siblings—they were all victims—for not doing more to put an end to his father's violence and abuse when he himself was only 13. Joar protested and tried to put a stop to the violence, but has since thought he should have done more. He even feels shame about the early abuse he himself was forced to endure. Terje, who describes himself as a very shy and easily embarrassed child, had a sense of shame in his teens, feeling sure that everyone could see what he had been subjected to (i.e. sexual assault) and that he was like an open book. He describes how he almost always went about with downcast eyes as a teenager.

According to research in the field, common consequences of violence and abuse in childhood include problems with attachment, social avoidance, sleep disorders, problems with concentration and aggression, as well as anxiety (Braarud and Nordanger 2011; Glad et al. 2010).

Self-Esteem, Alcohol and Drugs

All the men interviewed describe having low self-esteem. They have all, in their different ways, struggled with a sense of never being good enough. Even those men in our study who were subjected to partner violence describe experiencing a sense of inadequacy and feelings of worthlessness. The majority of men, although not all, who have been subjected to sexual abuse have also used alcohol, analgesics, anabolic steroids, cannabis and/or other drugs to deal with their sense of worthlessness and other difficult emotional issues. In many cases they were already surrounded by alcohol, and occasionally even drugs, as they grew up.

One of Erlend's earliest memories is of sitting on top of the freezer drinking beer while his father talked on the phone. His father permitted this. Erlend's developmental environment was dominated by regular partying and alcohol. He was only 4 or 5 years old the first time he got drunk at a party. The little boy was so drunk that he could no longer walk straight, but staggered around and fell over. Everybody at the party laughed and found this funny. Although this case is extreme, the easy availability and presence of alcohol (sometimes even drugs) seem extremely common in these men's backgrounds.

The abuse of various substances, with a stimulating or sedative effect, is something that is also found later in these men's lives, for shorter or longer periods. At very least we see the use of alcohol in certain situations in order to cope with insecurity and anxiety (for example, in larger social situations). Arne describes how he started drinking regularly after suffering abuse as a 12-year-old. By the age of 16 he had probably already been held in police cells ten times for being drunk. When he was 21 years old he became a long-term drug abuser. Erlend followed a similar drug abuse career, consuming alcohol from the age of 15 onwards. After a few years he was also using hash, amphetamines, cocaine and other drugs ("I tried everything"). Fortunately, he succeeded in giving up these drugs at the age of 29. Kjartan explains that he started getting drunk when he was only 12 or 13. Now, despite having received treatment for drug use, he still, at the age of 36, struggles not to fall back into his old habits.

Although the majority of the ten men interviewed have abused alcohol/drugs for longer or shorter periods, it should be noted that some have not, or that their use of alcohol has been at a normal and socially acceptable level. There are other men in our study who also display the tendency—albeit not as accentuated or prominent—to drink in order to ease the pain and avoid distressing thoughts.

Social Consequences

Being the victim of violence and abuse early in life often causes various social limitations in the future. According to contemporary psychological research concerning attachment (Bowlby 1994; Wennerberg 2010), as well as psychoanalytic studies of the significance of relationships (Stern 1995; Mitchel 1988) and research on trauma in various fields including neurology (Scaer 2001; Scaer 2005; Gerge 2010; van der Kolk 2014), we now know a great deal about the impact of a child's early relationships with their parents and other close caregivers on their relationships in adulthood (Bunkholdt 2000).

Just as there is an increased risk of psychological problems for a child who suffers sexual abuse, violence, bullying, harassment or neglect, there is also an increased risk that the child's future social relationships will be adversely affected. Our adult relationships tend to reflect our primary, emotionally significant relationships, particularly with close caregivers. It is not that, in an over-determined way, later relationships take on precisely the same pattern as our very first social experiences, but there is often a link.

The adult relationships of the men interviewed have often been influenced by the abuse and other forms of violence and neglect they have experienced in childhood, albeit in varying ways: difficulty in trusting other people (which is heightened if these people resemble the perpetrators of the abuse or are of the same gender) is both striking and common. Difficulties with close and intimate relationships in particular are a recurring theme, as well as a marked unease in various social situations. Arne says, for example, that he has many acquaintances but few real friends, and that he now has just one really good friend. Beyond that, Arne describes friends and family as a bit of a "fantasy". Erlend's statement is very telling: "I didn't let anyone in. I had such high walls. No one was allowed in, I shut down my feelings."

Some men who as boys were abused by men may now have very difficult relationships with men in particular. Bjarnar describes this:

> Well, it's probably this thing of trusting people, especially men. I didn't have too many friends back then … the mates I have today, of course, I met them in childhood, but I've probably burned lots of bridges and kept people at bay. …
> Interviewer: Is it easier with women?
> Probably, not consciously, but unconsciously, yes. I feel that it's easier to trust women than men. I have more female friends than male.

In a reverse example, Odd who was subjected in childhood to abuse by a woman, says he has always been afraid of women and has difficulty relating to them. His experiences with girls as a teenager were also bad. Odd also suggests that his social relationships in general are not altogether easy: "decent people don't want nothing to do with me". He thinks he sends out signals to, and is also drawn to, those "who are far from being God's chosen."

The patterns that emerge are not entirely unambiguous, however. Joar explains that despite his being subjected to abuse by his biological father and other forms of violence by his two stepfathers, it is primarily in his relationships to female partners that he experiences difficulties.

Terje also describes a life marked by loneliness: throughout childhood and adulthood he has been intensely lonely and has few friends. He has never had a girlfriend or lived with anyone. One of the men who abused him in childhood had said repeatedly while abusing him that this was something people did when they "felt affection for each other". Because Terje's experience was so frightening, loving or liking another person seemed equal to subjecting them to abuse. The consequence was a generalised fear of emotional closeness and physical intimacy.

Sexual abuse often occurs within particular kinds of social context, frequently within dysfunctional families and communities. However, one should not be too quick to conclude that all these men belong to one social group. As was pointed out by the director of one of the centres with which we collaborated, what the men who seek help have in common is that they have suffered periodic ill health and/or mental illness, as well as other negative consequences of the abuse to which they been victim. But, according to the director, they are not ill in the usual sense. They have PTSD and have grown up in situations that are characterised by neglect of care.

Several of the men have obviously grown up in unstable and sometimes broken families. A clear indicator of this is that so many of them mention siblings who have also been abused and have experienced similar difficulties, or have struggled with various mental health problems. Joar witnessed his brother being sexually abused by a family member. His brother was 10 before he began to speak. Terje has one brother and two sisters; one was diagnosed as bipolar, the other committed suicide five years ago. His brother has also sought help at the same centre for sexual abuse as Terje has. Erlend's siblings too have had severe problems. Although Erlend stopped his heavy abuse of drugs years ago and has since started to put his life in order, his older brother's life remains hampered by drug abuse and he is dependent on help from social services. In the case of Kjartan, the extent of the siblings' shared social legacy is even more pronounced: out of four children, three brothers are now drug addicts. Nevertheless, several other of the interviewees are clearly from more stable families.

A clear indicator of the negative social impact here is the emotional distance from others and the occasional self-imposed isolation common to many trauma victims—whether traumatised in childhood or adulthood. War veterans and others diagnosed with PTSD, or those who suffer from other mental illnesses due to traumatic events, often choose to live in isolated places, separate themselves off from others or exhibit other social problems (Ruzek et al. 2004; see also Scaer 2005, Figley and Nash 2007; Tick 2005). This is also evident in our material, with several of the men showing a tendency to isolate themselves, to retreat or to avoid certain social situations or activities. Or, as Sølve describes it, he feels fine at a conference while the focus is purely on work:

> … but in the evenings I give the socialising a miss. Because then I'm completely lost, I don't know what to do, so I might just as well sit alone in my room rather than sitting down there alone.
>
> Researcher: Do you feel distant or alienated to other people?
>
> Yes, I get—I don't find it's easy to suss out whether people like me or not. Then I get suspicious. Naturally I've developed a very well-functioning radar for people I should avoid and people I should mix with …. In a way I can spot them from afar. But at the same time I can see that my barriers, my comfort zone—I've built up barriers so as to feel secure. And everything that's between there and there—I lose out on because I display—I get evasive, instead of forthcoming, people give up on me, I withdraw.

As we have seen, the lives of these men are affected and dictated in adulthood in many ways by the violent experiences they have had as children. In addition to problems with anxiety, guilt, shame and other difficult emotions, many have experienced problems with alcohol and drugs. Poor self-esteem seems to be the rule rather than the exception and often has negative and restrictive effects on these men's social relationships, albeit to varying degrees. Occasionally one glimpses an even more tangible link between painful childhood experiences and similar experiences in adulthood.

Early Vulnerability—Increased Risk of Destructive Relationships in Adulthood?

One question raised by these interviews is whether there might be a connection between early exposure to violence and sexual abuse, putting these men at greater risk than others of ending up in similar situations again in adulthood. The concept of reenactment is very familiar and has been discussed in psychotherapeutic literature since Freud's time, receiving renewed interest in the contemporary literature on trauma. There is a tendency in those who have suffered trauma to repeat very painful experiences over and over again, putting themselves in harm's way, despite the seemingly illogical and destructive nature of such behaviour (Scaer 2005; Thoresen and Hjemdal 2014). While our material is limited, some of the more interesting examples are worth a mention here to throw light on this subject.

Joar has been subjected to a great deal of psychological and even physical violence as an adult, including, on one occasion, being stabbed by his former partner. In his own words: "Because I consistently go after girls who don't feel good about themselves and then I think: OK, now I can help you fix things so you can have a better life." His last relationship (mentioned earlier) eventually became so destructive that Joar lost any interest in life and developed suicidal thoughts. Joar believes that this situation, which he did eventually get out of, came about because he allows himself to be oppressed by women too easily, something he would never allow a man to do. Joar reflects on the fact that his mother was abused by a family member as a child and went on to choose men who in their turn subjected Joar and his brother to abuse. He says: "I choose women who are no good, don't I, I continue on the same path."

Odd, who was subjected in childhood to sexual abuse by an adult woman, has been repeatedly sexually harassed by his mother-in-law, who exposed herself to him and made unwanted sexual advances, despite his asking her to leave him alone ("It's been a hell for me"). At the time of his interview, Odd has broken all contact with his mother-in-law for some years and refuses to meet her. As outlined earlier, his relationships especially to women involve a high level of fear, although he experiences social relationships in general as a complex area. Symptomatically, Odd lives with his partner in his country cabin.

Erlend reflects on the lack of boundaries prevalent in the environment in which he grew up, which was expressed most drastically perhaps in the sexual abuse to which he was subjected as a child. Erlend was introduced to inappropriate attitudes to sex, which he believes affected his sexuality as an adult, so that for a very long time his sexuality was disconnected from any emotion—he was obsessive yet totally indifferent. Even when, early on, he was in a long-term, stable relationship with a woman, he had casual sex with other women. Erlend describes how a few years prior to his interview, he had been locked in a threesome with a couple he knew. To his own surprise, Erlend got involved in a sexual act with the woman together with her very proactive boyfriend, without having really understood where it was going. He describes a particular sexual act which the other man carried out on the woman in his presence as both brutal and unpleasant, despite the woman having consented to the act. Afterwards Erlend felt a strong disgust and that he had somehow been abused again. He reflects on his inability to say no in this situation: "that psychological bind you get into" is connected to childhood abuse. In actual fact he had no desire to participate, but still allowed himself to be drawn into this sexual situation.

Sølve describes a complicated and increasingly troubling sexual relationship he had with a female colleague for a period of time. In retrospect, he describes this in terms of his having been subjected to abuse, ending up in the woman's claws and unable to leave the relationship. He says: "Because she played on the same strings as my mother, so I was in a relationship against my will or an abusive situation with her for two years." Eventually the situation got out of control and nearly pushed Sølve to suicide. It was only thanks to the help he received from the crisis centre that he was able to escape this destructive relationship and move on.

Avoidance, Hyper-Vigilance and Other Reactions to Trauma

Other specific difficulties that individual interviewees have had, which can be directly linked to the sexual abuse they suffered in childhood, include difficulties in eating certain foods, compulsive washing or recurring nightmares about past events. All these responses can be seen as indicators of traumatisation, and in the instances described above this is clearly the case. The kinds of situation or activity that other men in our study have avoided for similar reasons—because they involve physical contact or exposure which can be associated with their experiences of abuse—may include football, gymnastics, bathing in public swimming pools or intimate hygiene for others (e.g. through their work) or for themselves (e.g. dentist). Some men indicate that the abuse meant that they also developed an excessive need for control; that is, "hyper-vigilance". The latter involves an almost constant vigilance and excessive alertness to potential danger in one's surroundings. Former members of the military, for example, who have spent long periods in war zones where they have been obliged to pay close attention to hostile activities and movements, can develop hyper-vigilance. However, traumatised people who have been subjected to prolonged psychological or physical abuse may exhibit similar symptoms, even when they are no longer in a situation where they are exposed to such dangers. Hyper-vigilance means that the central nervous system of the sufferer is overactive, a form of stress which is constantly switched on (Figley and Nash 2007, 50ff; Scaer 2001, pp. 79, 86, 99).

In several cases, the interviewees describe encounters with someone who looked like their abuser, triggering a powerful sense of unease. Terje, who recently encountered a flasher at a party, was so strongly reminded of his childhood abuser and so overwhelmed that he blacked out. He woke up in the hospital, but blacked out again when he was leaving. When Terje actually encountered his childhood attacker in a shop, it was, he says, as though the entire room froze, from floor to ceiling, and as though everything closed in on him, "like a fog". Terje quickly exited the store, terrified of meeting the man face to face.

Ola, who suffered as a child from neglect, repeated physical violence and was also subjected to sexual abuse, said he learned to dissociate early. Although Ola has occasionally had unpleasant memories and flashbacks, he has not experienced much anxiety or any strong sense of discomfort. Instead, the abuse has generated an internal flight mechanism in him, a tendency to consciously remove himself mentally. Already as a child, therefore, Ola became fearless and a risk-taker. And when he was with friends he got a kick out of challenging security guards and other adults, for instance by climbing over roofs or getting them to chase him. His propensity for risk-taking eventually led Ola to a successful military career and later a criminal career.

Terje imagined that he was someone else when he was subjected to abuse. He says that by obliterating his own self, the pain diminished.

Joar says that he is very capable of "closing myself off completely and doing nothing and just staring straight ahead of me". Asked if this is like having tunnel vision, he confirms that this is correct. Erlend says that he was not really troubled by anxiety or painful memories or images, rather that they were "shut down and locked away". He had done the same with the sexual abuse as he now did with any unpleasant experience: "I'd only done what I did with everything, put it behind me and forgot it, we don't talk about it any more, so it didn't happen." Kjartan also managed for a long time to suppress the extensive sexual abuse to which he had been exposed from early childhood to puberty. But later, when his suppressed memories suddenly returned to him in adulthood, he had a substantial crisis, during which he suffered severe anxiety and panic attacks.

All of the above reactions and symptoms described by our interviewees are possible symptoms of PTSD. While this may not be the explanation for all of them, and they may instead be linked to other conditions, it should be noted that some of the men have been diagnosed with PTSD.

Suicidal Thoughts

According to studies investigating the link between exposure to trauma or neglect in childhood and various forms of ill health in adulthood, suicide and suicide attempts are considerably more common in the exposed group than in a normal sample of the population (Felitti et al. 1998). In a meta-analysis of available research on the consequences of sexual abuse, Paolucci et al. (2001) found that sexual abuse in childhood or adolescence results in a significant risk of suicide. Studies of PTSD show the same. A stark illustration of this comes from US war veterans. In recent years during which the US Army had a large, active presence in Afghanistan and Iraq, more soldiers were lost through suicide than died in battle. These deaths often happen after the soldiers have left the battle zone, sometimes long after their actual military service.

A similar vulnerability caused by childhood experiences is also seen among our interviewees. Suicidal thoughts have been found in the majority of them, whether these have been constantly present or only for shorter periods. Although not all of the ten men report recurrent or periodic thoughts of taking their lives, the frequent occurrence of this in the material says something about the severity of the suffering that abused men carry with them.

Erlend was only 16 years old when he first thought that he might just as well die, because he felt he had "no purpose" in life. Joar says with reference to his poor self-esteem and lack of self-confidence that he sometimes had huge doubts about the meaning of life: "so I can just go and jump into the sea, simple". Odd, too, describes his sense of failure as leading to similar thought patterns. Sometimes, when he was driving a car and came towards a lorry, he would think that it would be better if it drove straight into him, as long as it was over quickly. He describes how at such moments he would just think: "come on, come on!" Instead of braking, he would put his foot on the accelerator. For periods of time Odd has seriously contemplated and even made detailed plans to take his own life, but has never been able to go through with it.

Kjartan suffered a severe mental breakdown five years before the interview. The memory of the abuse, which had previously gone from his mind, suddenly resurfaced with accompanying emotions and leaving him unable to sleep. Kjartan eventually attempted to kill himself, an impulse which has occasionally returned since.

References

Bowlby, J. (1994). *En trygg bas. Kliniska tillämpningar av anknytningsteorin.* orig. A Secure Base 1988. Stockholm: Natur & kultur.

Braarud, C. H., & Nordanger, D. Ø. (2011). Kompleks traumatisering hos barn: En utviklingspsykologisk forståelse. *Tidsskrift for Norsk Psykologforening, 48*(10), 968–972.

Bunkholdt, V. (2000). *Utviklingspsykologi.* Oslo: Universitetsforlaget.

Felitti, V. J., Anda, R. F., Nordenberg, D., Williamson, D. F., Spitz, A. M., Edwards, V., Koss, M. P., & Marks, J. S. (1998). Relationship of Childhood

Abuse and Household Dysfunction to Many of the Leading Causes of Death in Adults: The Adverse Childhood Experiences (ACE) Study. *American Journal of Preventive Medicine, 14*(4), 245–258.

Figley, C. R., & Nash, W. P. (Eds.). (2007). *Combat Stress Injury. Theory, Research, and Management.* New York: Routledge.

Finkelhor, D., Ormrod, R. K., & Turner, H. A. (2007). Poly-Victimization: A Neglected Component in Child Victimization. *Child Abuse & Neglect, 31*(1), 7–26.

Gerge, A. (2010). *Trauma. Psykoterapi vid Posttraumatisk och dissociativ problematik.* Ludvika: Dualis.

Glad, K. A., Øverlien, C., & Dyb, G. (2010). *Forebygging av fysiske og seksuelle overgrep mot barn: En kunnskapsoversikt.* Oslo: Nasjonalt kunnskapssenter om vold og traumatisk stress (NKVTS). Retrieved from https://www.nkvts.no/content/uploads/2015/08/forebyggingavfysiskeogseksuelleovergrepmotbarn_kunnskapsoversikt3.pdf.

van der Kolk, B. (2014). *The Body Keeps the Score. Brain, Mind, and Body in the Healing of Trauma.* New York: Penguin Books.

Krug, E. (2002). *World Report on Violence and Health.* Geneva: World Health Organization. Retrieved from http://www.who.int/violence_injury_prevention/violence/world_report/en/.

Mitchel, S. A. (1988). *Relational Concepts in Psychoanalysis. An Integration.* London: Harvard University Press.

Mossige, S., & Stefansen, K. (2007). *Vold og overgrep mot barn og unge: En selvrapporteringsstudie blant avgangselever i videregående skole* (Vol. 20/2007, NOVA-rapport (trykt utg.)). Oslo: Norsk institutt for forskning om oppvekst, velferd og aldring.

Mossige, S., & Stefansen, K. (2016). *Vold og overgrep mot barn og unge: Omfang og utviklingstrekk 2007–2015* (Vol. 5/2016, NOVA-rapport (trykt utg.)). Oslo: Norsk institutt for forskning om oppvekst, velferd og aldring.

Mullender, A., Hague, G., Imam, U., Kelly, L., Malos, E., & Regan, L. (2002). *Children's Perspectives on Domestic Violence.* London: SAGE Publications.

Paolucci, E., Genuis, M., & Violato, C. (2001). A Meta-Analysis of the Published Research on the Effects of Child Sexual Abuse. *The Journal of Psychology, 135*(1), 17–36.

Ruzek, I., Curran, E., Friedman, M. J., et al. (2004). Treatment of the Returned Iraq War Veteran. In *Iraq War Clinician Guide* (2nd ed., Chap. 4). Websida/ Published: U.S. Department of Veteran Affairs & National Center for PTSD. Retrieved from http://www.globalsecurity.org/military/library/report/2004/Chapter_IV.pdf.

Scaer, R. C. (2001). *The Body Bears the Burden. Trauma, Dissociation, and Disease*. New York: The Haworth Medical Press.

Scaer, R. C. (2005). *The Trauma Spectrum. Hidden Wounds and Human Resiliency*. New York: W.W. Norton & Company.

Sogn, H., & Hjemdal, O. K. (2010). *Vold mot menn i nære relasjoner: Kunnskapsgjennomgang og rapport fra et pilotprosjekt*. Oslo: Norsk kunnskapssenter om vold og traumatisk stress (NKVTS). Retrieved from https://www.nkvts.no/content/uploads/2015/08/voldmotmenninarerelasjoner2.pdf.

Steinsvåg, P. Ø. (2007). Få slut på våldet—ett säkerhetsarbete för barn. Kap. 1. Eriksson, Maria (red.), *Barns som upplever våld. Nordisk forskning och praktik*. Stockholm: Gothia Förlag.

Stern, D. N. (1995). *Spädbarnets interpersonella värld ur psykoanalytiskt och utvecklingspsykologiskt perspektiv*. orig. The Interpersonal World of the Infant, 1985. Stockholm, Natur & kultur.

Strøm, I., Thoresen, O. K, Myhre, M., Wentzel-Larsen, T., & Thoresen, S. (2017). The Social Context of Violence: A Study of Repeated Victimization in Adolescents and Young Adults. *Journal of Interpersonal Violence*, 1–26. First Published April 5, 2017. Open access https://doi.org/10.1177/0886260517696867.

Thoresen, S., & Hjemdal, O. K. (2014). *Vold og voldtekt i Norge: En nasjonal forekomststudie av vold i et livsløpsperspektiv* (Vol. 1/2014, Rapport (Nasjonalt kunnskapssenter om vold og traumatisk stress: trykt utg.)). Oslo: Nasjonalt kunnskapssenter om vold og traumatisk stress. Retrieved from https://www.nkvts.no/rapport/vold-og-voldtekt-i-norge-en-nasjonal-forekomststudie-av-vold-i-et-livslopsperspektiv/.

Tick, E. (2005). *War and the Soul. Healing Our Nations Veterans from Post-Traumatic Stress Disorder*. Wheaton: Quest Books.

Wennerberg, T. (2010). *Vi är våra relationer: Om anknytning, trauma och dissociation* (We Are Our Relations. On Attachment, Trauma and Dissociation). Stockholm: Natur & kultur.

Open Access This chapter is licensed under the terms of the Creative Commons Attribution 4.0 International License (http://creativecommons.org/licenses/by/4.0/), which permits use, sharing, adaptation, distribution and reproduction in any medium or format, as long as you give appropriate credit to the original author(s) and the source, provide a link to the Creative Commons licence and indicate if changes were made.

The images or other third party material in this chapter are included in the chapter's Creative Commons licence, unless indicated otherwise in a credit line to the material. If material is not included in the chapter's Creative Commons licence and your intended use is not permitted by statutory regulation or exceeds the permitted use, you will need to obtain permission directly from the copyright holder.

7

Experience with Support Agencies

Help-Seeking and Needs

It is well documented in a number of surveys that few people who experience violence, regardless of the relationships in which that violence occurs, actually seek help. As mentioned earlier, clinical trials of women (and men) who seek assistance as a result of intimate partner violence show that these victims suffer extensive physical injury and psychological damage. The men we interviewed who had sought help from crisis centres had been exposed to danger and saw no other way out. Several of the other men in our sample needed protection and experienced serious forms of violence.

Harald never approached a doctor or the police when he was physically harmed. He never talked about it with family or friends until after he had got out of the relationship. Tom did not seek medical attention before a friend confronted him about his injuries and asked him to call the doctor. The doctor then persuaded him to call the police. In his conversation with the police, they made it clear that he should report his partner for violence, but Tom did not because he wanted to protect his daughter. He

© The Author(s) 2019
M. I. Lien, J. Lorentzen, *Men's Experiences of Violence in Intimate Relationships*,
Palgrave Studies in Victims and Victimology,
https://doi.org/10.1007/978-3-030-03994-3_7

imagined a horrific scene in which the mother would be taken from their home by the police, and he refused to subject his daughter to that.

As previously outlined, men describe abuse that has contributed to anxiety and lack of self-esteem. Feelings of shame and self-loathing are frequent, as are concern for the children, caring for the partner, dependency on the partner and their partner's psychological control, which have all led to their not having left the relationship sooner. We have also seen that not everyone has experienced equally serious violence. Those men who have experienced milder forms of violence also report detrimental effects. However, an important finding in this section of the study is that the experience of systematic violence among the men in our study bears a marked similarity to that described in interviews with female victims of violence (Gottzén 2016; Coker et al. 2002; Tjaden and Thoennes 2000).

The men who have lived for a long time in violent relationships with women say that the women have had a psychological hold over them through a range of controlling behaviours and emotional abuse. These include ridicule, threats and humiliation. It seems particularly difficult for men to stand up against the latent threat of being deprived of their children and/or being accused of being violent themselves. The men we interviewed who have been subjected to systematic violence by female partners say that they needed, more than anything, to be believed. The relief at being understood and having the violence documented is highlighted by these men as an important and positive aspect of the encounter with crisis centres. Men who have been exposed to severe physical and psychological violence over time express a need for longer-term support from mental health teams, and the chance to talk to reorient themselves after the violence.

It is an ongoing theme in several other studies that men do not want to admit to being victims or that they try to hold on to a form of control linked to masculine values and self-image. This is not as clear in our study. In spite of the fact that it has taken time for these men to acknowledge that they have been exposed to various forms of violence, and that some of them trivialise the physical violence, we do not see any strong resistance to their acknowledging that they have been the victims of serious violent events.

The men we met in Chaps. 4 and 5 have sought help at crisis centres, family protection and other agencies such as the police, a GP, psychiatric organisations and child welfare. We will now see how men describe their encounter with these support agencies. We will look mainly at their experiences with family protection and crisis centres. We ask where and how they have sought help and their evaluation of the help they received. Additionally, in this chapter we look at these men's individual stories of seeking help, their encounter with the centres against incest and sexual abuse, and their evaluation of the help and support they have received.

At the Family Counselling Office

In Norway, couples therapy is offered by the family counselling service to married and cohabiting couples, as well as to couples who are in a romantic relationship but not living together. This service is available to both heterosexual and homosexual couples. Counselling may be sought because there are problems in the relationship or in connection with a breakup. All those who are married and have joint children under the age of 16 must obtain a valid mediation certificate before the County Governor can grant a separation or divorce. Cohabiting couples with joint children under the age of 16 must also attend mediation if they separate. A mediation certificate is required before the higher rate of child benefit will be granted. Parents who wish to petition the court for parental responsibility, permanent custody or contact rights must obtain a mediation certificate. The family counselling offices conduct statutory mediation. The aim of mediation is for the parents to come to an agreement about parental responsibility, permanent custody and contact. The primary purpose of any agreement relating to children is to safeguard the children's best interests.

The purpose of the family protection service is to intervene early where families are experiencing conflict and difficulties, offering them treatment and counselling. In Norway, family protection has a mandate to mediate according to the Marriage Act (section 26) and the Children's Act (section 51). Eight men in this study have had one or more meetings with family protection. Most were either summoned to a family protection office in connection with mediation due to the breakup of their relationship and/or arranged meetings on their own initiative in order to try to resolve conflicts after the breakup.

Albert and his wife attended a joint meeting to help establish future residence and a contact agreement for their two children. He explains that he did not think his ex-wife was a very good care provider and that he believed the children would do as well, if not better, with him after the breakup. He was largely the one who helped the children with their school work and saw to their social and physical activities. Since he contributed at least as much as his ex-wife in caring for the children, he wanted the children to live with him for the greater part or to share no less than 50 per cent of the parental responsibility. When he aired this possibility with his ex-wife and mentioned that he would suggest this to the family therapist, she threatened to take him to court. He said that he then chose to lie low at the meetings with family protection. We asked him how he experienced the talks they had with the family therapist:

> *I think the meeting with family protection was rather as expected. My wife wanted 60 per cent care. That was fine for family protection, but I didn't think it was reasonable because I was at least equal to her as a care provider. I just had to give it to her because she threatened me with going to court, and I ended up accepting 60 per cent care.*

To avoid problems, Albert signed the 40/60 agreement, despite the fact that he would have liked to have the children more. And in practice he does, but his wife still receives contributions from him as well as the full child benefit. He says that he knew there was no point in fighting for a 50 per cent division, because she "would have got what she wanted anyway".

As mentioned previously, family therapists have the important task of uncovering violence and power relationships between couples in conflict. After approximately ten years, Harald wanted to break out of his marriage, and he and his wife therefore had to attend mediation with family protection. However, when asked if he mentioned the fact that he had been subjected to violence by his wife, Harald answers:

I didn't say that I'd been subjected to violence. It wasn't a subject I touched on, but then, we weren't asked about it either. There weren't any one-to-one conversations where they tried to make it possible for the partners to open up.

According to Harald, mediation about contact and residence for the children was the only focus of their joint discussions with the family therapist. He and his wife had agreed that they should try to get shared parental care by moving in and out of the family home and another apartment they rented. We asked him why he could not tell the therapist about the violence.

Researcher: Why couldn't you say what you'd been subjected to?

My experiences were with me in that room of course, but I remember that when we came out of the mediation talks—my wife—she was smart, she was pretty, she presented as a resourceful woman, she could wind them around the little finger.

Researcher: What did you think about the situation, can you describe it?

Well. There are two women sitting there, my wife and a female family therapist, and then as a 30-year-old man I'm supposed to say: hey, I think my wife is psychologically abusive towards me. I assumed they'd think: oh, he's trying to get more parental rights now, you see. No. I didn't have the feeling that this was the right forum. Why would I say anything about it? I wouldn't have been believed anyway, you see. That's what I felt, plus the fact that—it's also about how conscious you are yourself—about what's going on. Because at that point I was very low. Any reality checks I had were blown out of the water, I thought I was totally and utterly worthless. That was the feeling I was sitting there with. A bit like: thank you for taking the time to mediate in the divorce between me and my crazy wife.

Harald believes that family protection contributed to hiding the violence because they were too concerned about being a neutral mediation body. In addition, he felt that his wife had the psychological upper hand and that she steered the discussions at the meetings. On the one hand, he assumed that no one would believe she subjected him to violence whatever he said. On the other, he felt that the family protection office was not a suitable forum in which to broach the subject of violence:

I think that by being neutral, one always has to listen to both sides of the case and try to reach some common understanding of things. Which means, in a way, that the only common understanding you'll get to, is that of the person who has the power in the relationship. … But if she'd wanted more [parental] care, I'd have been screwed. I'd have been fucked. No one would believe me.

Several men explain that they resign themselves because they feel powerless, and because they sense that the family therapists will neither understand nor believe their version of events and their experience of the family situation. A sense of powerlessness and fear of being subject to suspicion are also clear in Fredrik's narrative. As we shall see, it was his wife's situation and the challenge of controlling her anger towards the children which were the focus in their mediation talks.

Fredrik says that during the first mediation meeting he did not talk to the therapist about the systematic emotional abuse to which his wife subjected the children. Nor were the harassment, threats and physical violence towards him ever raised. In the second mediation meeting, Fredrik mentioned that his wife threw things at him and had threatened him with a knife, but he felt that the family therapist treated him "like a fly on the wall" (his expression). The focus of the discussion went entirely on strengthening the relationship between mother and children, because she was clearly "tired" and unstable. Nor did Fredrik ever mention the psychological violence in later mediation meetings with family protection. When asked why he did not say anything about this, he says: "I felt a lot of guilt and shame and wasn't going to bare my soul in a shared conversation with my wife and some unknown person." In addition, the family therapist had already trivialised the physical violence he had mentioned previously. He got the impression that the family therapist did not believe him, and he had therefore decided to avoid any problems by putting the topic to rest in future discussions.

During our interview with Fredrik, he asked if we wanted documentation on his case because he thought: "I'm sure this all sounds pretty weird, and that I'm completely nuts."

The interviews also show examples where family protection has met men with understanding of difficult relationships between mother and father. When Tor and his wife separated, they went to family protection for mediation. They had three meetings and received help in making a detailed

agreement about their daughter's residence. Tor felt that the family therapist saw his situation and acknowledged that his ex-wife was "difficult to
cooperate with". According to Tor, this meeting was the first time that he
had been taken seriously by a support agency, and the therapist contributed to the agreement for the care of their daughter being formalised:

> *They did what was right at an early phase of a breakup. They explained their
> task and aim to mediate in the best interests of the child. … I think they saw
> that she was the difficult party who was not ready to cooperate.*

Tor's problems came later, to which we will return. After the divorce
his wife took their daughter and moved a long distance away with no
prior warning.

Tom also met understanding at the initial meetings with the family
therapist when he contacted them saying that he was in "conflict" with
his partner. The meetings showed that his partner had difficulties controlling her temper. The therapist was helpful and solution focused. She suggested that Tom's partner could attend an anger management course run
by family protection, but the partner did not want help with her anger:

> *We were there about four times. It was very positive. The therapist there was a
> mature lady. She was very attentive, I remember. Eventually she told my part-
> ner that an offer has come through for an anger management course, and that
> she'd recommend her. Then my partner got up, walked out of the door and never
> returned.*

As previously mentioned, most of the men have experience of family
protection in the contexts of mediation. Family protection has the best
interests of the child in cases of conflict. Its aim is to help parents find the
best solution for the children by making contact orders.

She's the One Who Needs Help

Erik (52) does not have children with his current wife, but approached
family protection for help with their relationship. He primarily wanted
her to get help to deal with her aggression and feelings, and did not

inform the family therapists that he was being subjected to violence. This is one of several attempts by Erik to get help for his wife. She refuses to accept help, despite the fact that Erik believes she clearly needs support in handling some very difficult childhood experiences. After years of violent episodes and much arguing, Erik contacted the family protection office. For him, outside help was, and still is, a prerequisite to his being able to continue the relationship. His wife preferred not to participate in partner therapy or seek the help of family protection. At the time of the interview, Erik and his wife had had joint sessions with a family therapist about five times. We asked Erik if the violence had been a topic for discussion.

> Researcher: Have you talked to the therapist about what she is doing to you?
> Erik: *It has only been touched on, but we haven't come so far as to get into these things. It's still very superficial. We haven't talked about the violence problem. We can sort of mention that there have been episodes, but we haven't gone into any detail about what's happened. There are things that we don't really talk about at home because, once there's been an episode like that, you're completely broken and upset the next day. And then it's kinda easier not to talk about it, then next time, when you want to bring it up it just turns into an uncomfortable situation and everything just gets pushed under the carpet.*

As we can see, Erik speaks in terms of "we", even though *he* is the initiator of these discussions and the subject of various sorts of violence. At home he cannot bring up the subject of the violence with his wife, because doing so generally makes it worse. Erik has sometimes had to take sick leave as a result of the conflict and violent episodes at home. However, he has not asked for a one-to-one consultation with the therapist, nor does he want to focus on the violence, since he feels that his wife is the one who needs help. When asked if he believes the therapist suspects that his wife is unstable and violent, Erik answers as follows:

> *I don't know, but he [the therapist] is clever in a way at trying to avoid [talking about] some of these situations. When he observes us moving away from each other, we often end [the discussion]. Then we go on to talk about something more pleasant—so we can get closer.*

As we see, Erik feels that the therapist tries to bring them together. Since the therapist does not know how difficult things are at home, the focus remains on the positive things in the relationship. Erik says he loves his wife and wants to help her. He says he knows that their relationship will be destroyed if he tells family protection that she hits him and kicks him and is verbally abusive when she is drunk. He says he feels sorry for her and wants to protect her.

Erik has a high level of education. He is the sole provider and has a large professional and personal network. His wife has neither a job nor a social network in Norway. She has repeatedly threatened to call the crisis centre when they have argued. Despite being depressed and angry and feeling that the situation with his wife is often out of control, Erik says he would never consider contacting a crisis centre himself to talk. He is a white man with a good job, the main provider and married to a minority woman. Who would believe that he feared her or needed protection?

Clinical Conversations

Andreas describes a time when he approached family protection to make an appointment in order to come to an agreement with his ex-girlfriend about contact with his son:

I went to family protection just before my son's mother took him and moved away. My ex-girlfriend came to the meeting very reluctantly. But she was there and doubtless felt she was at war, since she seemed very nervous and on edge. She didn't agree to anything more than the bare minimum of contact—just to what she had to [agree to] not to have sabotaged it. I'd also sought help from family protection before. Very little came out of the meetings with family protection. My ex was sort of pushed into it and thought it was just bullshit. She felt it as an attack on the control she had.

Researcher: Did she deny that there was any reason for you both being there?

Yes. yes. There wasn't a problem in her eyes. Nothing in particular came out of those meetings. We were offered more sessions. I don't remember them having any power or authority to go into anything at all.

Andreas says that he spoke openly with the family therapist about how the mother of his son refused to allow him to participate in the care of the child, and how in many ways she sabotaged the contact between them. The family therapists stated that they could not offer anything more than advice. We asked if he felt that family protection understood his situation:

> *I don't really know if they were able to understand my situation because there were two explanations. Mine and hers. What I experienced was that all the agencies that had anything to do with parents and children worked only as advisors and they could try to steer things in a certain direction, but when one party exerts its power, it's useless. In my case, the mother had all the power.*

The latent threat of sabotage of their role as a father and of the switching of the violence relationship is central to the explanation several men give when telling us why they did not raise the subject of the violence with family therapists. The men's reticence in talking to relevant professionals about the violence must be seen in the light of the social and institutional contexts in which they find themselves. It is important to question whether support professionals have good enough tools to map out the forms of violence that may be perpetrated by women and mothers. There are, of course, limitations in our material when it comes to making generalisations about the various support agencies, but these men's stories can contribute to our understanding of why men remain silent about their experiences of violence.

The experience men have of meeting family protection is that staff either direct their professional and interpersonal focus to strengthening the mother–child relationship or appear to be so neutral that the problem of violence cannot be brought up.

Our interviews reveal that men have the words with which to describe their experiences and feelings. It is the fear of not being believed, or the perceived risk of being regarded as perpetrators themselves, which is why men do not talk to professionals or networks before they are physically injured or have a breakdown because of emotional abuse over time. Our interviews with men who have been helped by the crisis centres show that when these men encounter an environment where there is professional

competence in the field of violence against men and where staff are ready
to meet men and listen to their stories, men open up and accept help and
support.

The men who have children have various experiences of sabotage of
contact. Tor's ex-wife broke the contact order, took their daughter and
moved far away without telling him. Family protection has no mandate
to intervene in such a situation, and the couple ended up in a bitter conflict in the courts.

As previously mentioned, Andreas did not live with his ex-girlfriend,
making it possible for her to keep him in a marginal position in relationship to their son. The family therapist he spoke to was nice enough and
she went some way to acknowledging his frustrations, but, according to
Andreas, she could do nothing to help him in the disempowered situation he found himself in as a father. He describes how he experienced his
conversations with the family therapist:

> For me the whole situation was weird. I didn't know what to do. You meet a
> system that's designed to deal with violent men, bad fathers. They will make
> sure that the mother and child are protected. They aren't geared up to help a
> father who's a victim. So it's a pretty raw deal, in my opinion. You don't have
> anyone to go to for help.

In particular, those fathers who have lost access rights and/or been
subjected to the repeated threat of losing contact with their children have
experienced family protection as too passive, as having protected the
mother and/or adopted a neutral attitude to the experiences of violence
they have been told about.

The findings indicate that family protection has difficulty in uncovering women's violence.

As part of a preliminary project for this study, we interviewed three
family therapists with extensive experience in working with partner violence. We asked them how they worked with cases of family violence and
their experiences with couples where the man was the victim. The two
offices with whom we were in contact have a rule: if there is any suspicion
that violence is involved in the relationship, they arrange a meeting with
each partner separately. One of the challenges to have emerged is the

reluctance in men to talk about being the victim of violence. It is generally the woman who presents the problems in the relationship, and who largely controls the dialogue with the therapist. It is her understanding of the situation that dominates this dialogue and the man often remains silent, letting her define the relationship.

Our interviews can give some insight into why men and fathers exposed to different forms of violence do not speak about their problems. Their silence should not be solely linked to norms of masculinity and the notion that men lack the language for their experiences (Kimmel 2002; Seidler 1997). Men's silence can also be related to what is at stake in the family protection office—the risk of losing contact with children and the fear of switching of the violence and the dominating role.

The Wrong Sort of Victim

An experience which may be unique to men is the feeling of being the "wrong" sort of victim in the eyes of the support agencies, and a fear of not being believed when they first talk about their experiences. Men are still regarded as unacceptable victims of violence in intimate relationships (Kimmel 2002; Douglas et al. 2012). We have seen that men have both internal and external barriers to seeking help, and that those men who have been in contact with family protection and child protection find that the system has been set up to support abused women and/or mentally unstable mothers. A similar gender bias in support agencies is found in other interviews of men subjected to intimate partner violence (Machado et al. 2016; Corbally 2015). In a Portuguese survey of men subjected to intimate partner violence, Machado et al. (2016) found that men suffer in silence and that the risk of stigma, gender bias in the relevant agencies, together with strong internalisation of ideals about masculinity prevent them from seeking help. The cultural perception of family violence and masculinity contributes to the self-censorship of feelings and experiences when encountering therapists, but also affects men's relationships with friends and family. When family therapists have no sense of the "social game" (Bourdieu 2001), they risk becoming the co-creators of symbolic violence, in that they misconstrue cultural beliefs about mothers and the position of power that women occupy in this context as both legitimate and natural (Bourdieu and Passeron 1977, pp. 5–6).

Family protection and child welfare are the bearers of hegemonic discourses about violence and parenthood. Fear of switching of the violence and the perpetrator role must be seen in the light of established discourse about family violence both within and outside the institutions the couple find themselves in.

Crisis Centres for Men

In Norway there are 43 crisis centres for men. In 2016 there were 131 men living in Norwegian crisis centres. The numbers of men and nights of stay have remained relatively stable in comparison with the figures for 2014 and 2015, but represent a considerable increase from before 2010, when a law was passed making it mandatory for crisis centres to be made available to men. Prior to 2010 crisis centres were open only to women, just as they usually are across the world. They were organised differently, run by voluntary organisations or by local councils. When the law was passed instituting the right of access to crisis centres, it became gender neutral, as indeed all laws are in Norway, and it was also made mandatory to offer services locally for male victims of violence.

The offer of crisis centres is therefore aimed at all those who are vulnerable to violence in intimate relationships; that is, both women and men, the elderly, children (with their caregivers), young people, disabled people, members of the LGBT community (lesbians, gays, bisexuals and transvestites).

Some crisis centres offer either free and temporary accommodation which is available 24 hours a day, every day of the year, while others have a daytime service offering one-to-one counselling and the opportunity to join support groups. No referral is required to get into a crisis centre and users can remain anonymous if they wish.

Experiences of Help from Crisis Centres

Most of the men interviewed express huge satisfaction with the help they have received from crisis centres and the centres against incest and sexual assault. Some, however, are less satisfied and have suggestions for improvement, something to which we will return. Nevertheless, the overall picture is that crisis centres have in many ways been crucial to these men's view of themselves, and their understanding of what they have been subjected to and how they can move on in life. Both the Norwegian men and those from minority backgrounds are largely pleased with the offer. This generally tallies with the findings of the report *Menn på krisesenter* (*Men at Crisis Centres*; Grøvdal and Jonassen 2015, p. 73) and differs from findings in previous studies about men's experiences with other services (Machado et al. 2016).

Arild says he is "very pleased" with his stay at the centre. Bashir says that "they were really welcoming, and it was safe too". Deo emphasizes that "they have helped me a lot, and they are very kind". Ali says that "I was looked after really well, it was good to feel that there was someone who could help you in this difficult situation."

When we ask Jonas what he thinks about the help he received, he says:

> *I probably wouldn't be here today without their help. Actually, the most important thing they did for me was to help me see what kind of life I'd lived. It took a long time before I could admit that there had been something called violence from her side. They also taught me—they spent a lot of time telling me off, unbelievably, they taught me where my responsibility begins and where it ends. I can't take responsibility for the things she does, least of all the things she does when I'm not there.*
>
> Researcher: They really helped you through then?
>
> *Yes, I don't think I'd have managed this without them, looking back that's what I think—if I'd managed without them, I don't think I'd have been a very good person today, especially towards women. It was really positive because—as I said I know some men in the same situation, I see some of them around. Many of them are real women-haters. I see abused women who are man-haters, and it's very easy to fall into that. But despite everything it was women who welcomed me, and it's women I've talked to.*

Jonas feels that he has a completely different understanding of himself and of what he went through after his stay at the crisis centre. He is glad he went there because it was touch and go, according to him. First his mother almost forced him to make contact, then she drove him down and left him on the steps outside. He met an acquaintance, who already lived there, but he told her he was not thinking of staying, he just wanted to take a look. But then he told her his story and she started pulling him up the steps. Jonas says:

> *Then she started to pull me and wanted to drag me up the steps and I held back. I said: you won't get me in there, not at least—I know you live here, you're not going to get me in there. Then she rang the doorbell and a member of staff came out, she pulled me up straight and pushed me in through the door. But I was so sure that this place, that it wasn't for me, I was scared I'd be accused of something and that I'd have to listen to how nice my wife was.*

When he entered the therapy room he was shaking so much that he spilled his coffee. He was terrified. Jonas did not want to talk about the violence and with that show his own vulnerability. He was also afraid he would not be believed. Jonas says that he was afraid that they would say that his wife was sweet and nice and that he was the problem. So deeply engrained is the idea of who the perpetrator of violence is in a relationship between a man and woman that men who are exposed to it assume that they will never be believed. It may also have been the notion of a "sisterhood" that many people connect with crisis centres which increased Jonas's fear.

The crisis centre was also of vital importance to Peter, and he too found it difficult to make the first contact:

> *Before I came here, it felt very humiliating, it really did. But on the other hand, when I came here for the first time, and rang on the doorbell, and went up to the conversation room, it was like losing 1000 kilos from off my shoulders. It was such a relief to be able to sit there. They said I could sleep there. It was lovely because then I felt so free. To me it was like sitting in heaven.*

The combination of uncertainty as to what they are going into, their general lack of knowledge about the crisis centre and the fact that they were met with such professionalism and caring is central to these men's interpretation of their encounter with the crisis centre. They have low, or even no, expectations, or in Jonas's case negative expectations. When they are met with support and recognition, it is like arriving in "heaven". In many ways the men we interviewed from the crisis centre see themselves as the lucky ones who found their way there; they are grateful that someone would talk to them at all and take them seriously.

Problems with Separate Accommodation and Inadequate Help

Carlos (22) is in a slightly unusual situation in that he is an adult, but came to the crisis centre with his mother and brother. The whole family had been subjected to violence by the father and the stepfather. According to the Norwegian Crisis Centre Act, men and women must be accommodated in separate areas of the centre. Carlos's story illustrates challenges in how crisis centres are organised. Since he was over 18, he had to live on his own in the men's section, rather than with his mother and younger brother. The men's section is physically separate from the women's and there were no other men living at the centre during the weeks he spent there, so Carlos was alone. His mother was allowed to visit him in the men's section, while Carlos could not visit his mother in the women's section. This shows how problematic the segregation of men and women can be. Because Carlos was defined as a man, he could not set foot in the women's section and participate in any family activities that were arranged there. Nonetheless, Carlos is very pleased with the professional help he received:

> Researcher: You came to the crisis centre as a young adult. Did they take care of you too, or did they only take care of your mother? That's an important question for me.
>
> *Yes, I really felt that when they talked with me, I was the focus, and of course there was talk about the whole situation, but they wanted to take care of me. They came up with some ideas—that perhaps I could live on my own and be more self-reliant because I was going to take some exams and so forth. That wasn't what I wanted, but at least they wanted to safeguard my interests separately to my mother. I felt they were thinking like that.*

Researcher: Yes, because the situations you've been through for years are pretty traumatic?

Yes.

Researcher: So it was important to address that too, to look at it.

I felt they helped me with that. Yes. It was amazingly kind that such an offer exists. What would have happened [without it]? What would we have done? It was absolutely amazing. Really.

The staff at the centre recognised that Carlos had taken a huge amount of responsibility in the situation—for both his mother and his younger siblings—and they encouraged him to take care of his own needs. Their support became extremely important to him. At the same time, gender-divided accommodation meant that he was excluded from his family's everyday life and he had no other men in the same situation to talk to. Several other interviewees also suggested that separate accommodation could have an unfortunate impact on social relationships and eventual rehabilitation. Peter says that the women had a barbecue one evening, which he was not allowed to attend. Instead, the staff came in with some barbecued food for him. Peter thought this was boring and rather a shame, and he did not understand why he could not join in. "We could actually have had something to talk about. They (the women) come here for similar reasons to me," he comments. From the men's perspective— "we're all in the same boat"—the statutory segregation of the sexes can seem inappropriate and a constructed distinction.

Ali also reflects on this difference. He thinks it would be good if the women and men could meet for some hours in the afternoon and if some mealtimes could be shared. "Why couldn't we eat our meals together?" he asks. Ali, too, is far from dissatisfied with his stay, but thinks that improvements could be made. He also says that he feels there are differences in the way women and men are treated: "the women here get help quickly and straight away".

Most of the men who came to the centre lived there alone and had to manage for themselves. The fact that the men are isolated from a larger community at the centre represents a continuation of the loneliness these men experienced before arriving there. Considering the vulnerability of their situation, we consider this to be problematic.

The clearest criticisms of the treatment at the crisis centre come from Zaid and Daniel. When Daniel called the council's crisis centre and asked for help, he was told that "the only offer they had was for women". Although Daniel had nowhere to live, he was not allowed to stay at the centre, nor was he informed that the council had a duty to find him a place. The crisis centre asked him to contact the Red Cross or a similar organisation. Daniel is perhaps one of the men in our research who was subjected to the most extensive violence, and he has no explanation as to why he was turned away by the crisis centre.

The centre also promised to call him back, but failed to do so. Daniel was extremely disappointed about this, but he was fortunate enough to be offered excellent help from Skeiv verden[1] when he contacted them. Daniel is also the only interviewee who says that he cannot advise other men to contact the crisis centre.

Zaid was very impressed by the "fantastic" help he was getting at the crisis centre, until, when he had been there for four weeks, he was suddenly informed that he would have to move out the following day. This came as a huge shock to him and his situation worsened substantially as a result. He was told by the crisis centre to approach Norwegian Labour and Welfare Administration (NAV), who would find him a place to stay. The whole experience of being thrown out led him to say in his interview that he is now in a terrible state and "hates everything". Zaid feels that the centre gave him poor information and he does not understand why he could not live there any longer.

The positive feedback we received from these men about their experiences with crisis centres proved to apply equally to men who sought help from incest centres.

Centres Against Incest and Sexual Abuse

In Norway there are 19 centres against incest and sexual abuse. They are all are open to men. One of the centres only offers its services to men. The statistics have always shown that the majority of the users of centres against incest and sexual abuse are women and girls. By 2016, 82 per cent

---

[1] Skeiv verden is a national organization for LGBT people with minority background in Norway.

of users who had suffered sexual abuse (from both family and non-family members) were women and 18 per cent were men. The distribution of genders has been relatively stable over time. The percentage of men varied from 16 per cent to 20 per cent between 2009 and 2016. Among the male users who were victims the average age was 39 years, as opposed to 34 years for women. Of those users who were aged 50 and above, almost 3 out of 10 were men. The figures show that it usually takes longer for men to get to the stage where seeking help becomes a possibility: 54 per cent of men were subjected to abuse for the first time when they were between 7 and 15 years old. Only 16 per cent of men say that they reported the relationship and 11 per cent of the male victims had applied for criminal injuries compensation. Later in this chapter we investigate men's experience of the help they have received from support centres. We will now turn our focus to the experiences reported by men of talking/conversation therapies and other contact with professionals as well as activities offered by these centres.

Experiences with Conversation Therapies and Other Help

The experiences reported by the men from the two centres against sexual abuse that participated in our study are overwhelmingly and unambiguously positive. The staff at these two centres are highly valued and appreciated by the men we interviewed. It is not rare for the men to describe their encounter with these centres as a crucial turning point, a moment when their lives began to go in a more positive direction.

Bjørn (48) had never spoken to anyone (not even his former partner) about the abuse to which he had been subjected aged 11, before he contacted one of the centres in 2014. This meant that Bjørn had carried his memories inside him for 35 years without talking to anyone about them. In the end, however, the need to talk about the abuse with someone became so strong that it could no longer be ignored: "It was like something gnawing was at my stomach, and it felt like I was going to faint … I felt nauseous." He searched the internet and found the centre. This was to be a turning point for him: "All honour and glory to those who work here, they are fantastically clever people!" His contact with the support centre has since enabled Bjørn to tell, among other people, his daughter, his doctor and his boss what he went through as a child. He says he was well treated and got various kinds of support, which were all excellent.

Terje claims to have had little or no real help earlier in dealing with the sexual abuse in his childhood. He contacted the centre through his brother and feels he received good treatment there. The continuous contact with the centre has helped Terje to lighten the consequences of his childhood abuse, and even to render his appalling past harmless.

Arne, as mentioned earlier, was subjected to sexual abuse by his football trainer when he was 12. The abuse was discovered and the perpetrator was tried and convicted. Nevertheless, Arne feels that it was only when he came into contact with the centre that he received any real help in dealing with his experiences. Before coming to the centre he was about to give up, since there seemed little chance of getting help anywhere. So this was Arne's last hope (he was referred by his GP). He is full of praise for the treatment he received at the centre and says that the experience has been nothing but positive. He says his female conversation partner is amazing, that his needs have been "totally" met and that his time with the centre represents a turning point in his life. Erlend is also full of praise for the centre and its staff. He describes his contact with the centre as "completely amazing. It was unbelievably good to come here."

On a scale of one to ten, Odd gives the centre he visits a ten. Here he meets understanding, is accepted as he is and is given the help he needs to think more clearly and in new ways about himself and his difficult experiences. Odd is emphatic when he says that the help he received there made it possible for him to go on with his life and gave him back a sense of joy.

At first Sølve was sceptical and reticent about the activities and opportunities he was offered, but has become increasingly positive over time: "The centre works for me 100 per cent. Yes."

Many men mention the importance of talking to another man about their experiences of abuse. For those who have been abused by women, having a male talking partner can be essential. One or two men suggest that the gender of the person they meet to talk about their experiences is irrelevant or, indeed, that they feel more comfortable talking to a woman. Most, however, prefer to talk to a man and also emphasise the importance of this being a man with similar experiences to their own. This contributes to the sense of being heard, seen and understood. In contrast to the formal support available, Odd (63) insists that "the guys here have [hands-on] knowledge, they know [about it] from their own experience". Joar (28) says that "it's amazingly good to have someone to talk to as an adult, especially a man who might also have experienced stuff". Joar says he would have come to the centre earlier if he had known the quality of the help he would get there.

The importance of being received quickly after you have taken the very difficult step of ringing or visiting the centre is also highlighted. It is essential that the men are not left to stand in a queue or made to wait their turn. The unbureaucratic organisation and spirit of these centres appear therefore to be as important as the experience of being really understood and respected. The importance of being seen quickly and easily, and received with open arms without any expectation or judgement, is also crucial to the positive experience offered at these centres.

Given the positive impact these centres have had, and continue to have, on the lives of our interviewees, it is important to identify how they found out about the centres' activities and how they came into contact with them. Most of them seem to have had only the vaguest knowledge, or no knowledge at all, of the various activities run by the centres. They have quite simply been driven to attend by the overwhelming need to talk about the sexual assaults to which they have been exposed, often in childhood: difficult and/or painful experiences that they have never previously shared with anyone or, for that matter, received any professional help in processing. Often it is a current crisis in life, such as a divorce or other marital problem, which is the trigger. But it can also be the accumulated weight of painful experiences, which eventually becomes impossible to bear. Sometimes it can be a small, yet significant incident that triggers memories and symptoms linked to the abuse.

In three cases, it was someone close (partner, sibling) who tipped the men off about the centres' existence and the chance of their getting help there. Three were referred by other professional agencies or persons (staff members of other crisis centres, e.g. doctors). Three others found information after looking on the internet, while one found out about it in a short article.

Summary and Recommendations for an Improved Support System

Earlier studies indicate that negative childhood experiences are one of the main causes of ill health in adulthood (Felitti et al. 1998; Felitti 2003). These studies also indicate that various types of difficulties accumulate and increase the risk. Factors that contribute to an increased vulnerability are, among other things, physical and sexual violence, emotional neglect, the divorce of parents, and parents suffering with mental illness and/or alcohol problems. Previous studies have, as mentioned earlier, also shown that people who have experienced violence from others are at increased risk of partner violence (Haaland et al. 2005, p. 54).

In this study we find that many of the men who have been in contact with the centres against incest and sexual abuse because of their child-hood experiences of violence and sexual abuse have also experienced violence in adulthood. Those men who have been subjected to sexual assault have generally also been subjected to other forms of physical violence, bullying, psychological violence or neglect. Of the men in our study subjected to partner violence, there are several who say they were also subjected to bullying and other violence as children and/or teenagers; this is particularly true in the case of men from immigrant backgrounds. However, several of the men describe a stable and secure childhood.

The consequences of violence vary in gravity and depend on its extent and duration. But the consequences of sexual abuse and other forms of violence are very often wide reaching and profound: shame, guilt and fear are common, as are low self-esteem, suicidal thoughts and alcohol or drug abuse. Other common reactions and symptoms in men, which can more specifically be linked to trauma, are anxiety, panic attacks, depression, sleeping difficulties, phobias, avoidance of situations reminiscent of the abuse, elevated stress levels, hyper-vigilance and dissociation.

For many of the men in our study, abuse and violence have also had social consequences, including lack of confidence, loneliness, tendencies towards isolation and problems with close or intimate relationships. The men who have been subjected to violence and abuse have often taken time before being able to acknowledge and deal with the violence of which they have been a victim. Years have frequently gone by before these men reached out to any support agencies. Interviews we have conducted with staff within family protection, crisis centres and centres against incest and sexual abuse reflect the findings of prevalence studies—that most men wait a long time to approach healthcare services, the police or other professionals when they experience violence. By the time they seek help, the violence has generally been going on for a long time.

Nordic and international studies have found that men who are exposed to physical and mental abuse by a partner suffer similar physical and psychological damage to that experienced by women (Grøvdal and Jonassen 2015; Helweg-Larsen and Frederiksen 2008; Sogn and Hjemdal 2009; Hines and Douglas 2011, 2015; Hines et al. 2001; Coker et al. 2002). The right kind of help from support agencies can help reduce the negative health effects of violence in intimate relationships and contribute to helping both victims and their children. Being believed is essential to receiving help. Our interviews with men who have experienced partner violence perpetrated by women suggest that women/mothers have a privileged position within the system: that they can sabotage contact, threaten court action and/or the switching of the violence and power relationship. Those offering help must understand that men who are the main providers and in full-time employment can live with serious violence from women.

Encounters with various professional bodies—such as the DPS (local psychiatric units), medical profession, psychologists, police or schools—are often described in these interviews as inadequate or negative. Despite examples to the contrary, the men in our sample have often felt that they have not been listened to; they have even been ignored and occasionally misdiagnosed.

A common experience among most of the fathers in our study is that they feel that family protection and other organisations spend more time supporting mentally unstable mothers than assessing the father's resources and ability to offer care. The men find that parts of the government support system, such as family protection, have a gender bias and that staff subject them to indirect abuse by taking the side of violent mothers. Several of our interviewees say they have had no legal protection as fathers. However, our sample is not large enough for us to claim that these men's experiences represent a widespread trend among men who are in contact with family protection in Norway.

It is also important to point out that the majority of our interviewees who have been users of family protection had no contact with family therapists until late in the process—that is, in situations of high-level conflict and relationship breakdown. We have found that men often feel that support agencies are oriented towards traditional gendered beliefs about men and women. This is in line with other studies. In a Norwegian interview study of minority men's encounters with family protection, it was found that the views of staff were coloured by just such traditional assumptions about men and women, and that such prejudices almost automatically led staff to take the side of the woman (Lopez 2007, pp. 10–11). Looking at these studies in context, we can infer that the official support system has difficulty in addressing men's vulnerability and their need for help in these difficult situations in their lives, and that this must be seen in the light of dominant gendered ideas and understanding of "violence" and "victims".

Surveys carried out in the present study have also documented that the support system appears to be lacking in knowledge about the services available to men subjected to violence in intimate relationships. These findings may indicate that the system has problems identifying male victims and/or not recognizing when men require help.

A pilot study on violence against men in intimate relationships (Sogn and Hjemdal 2009) revealed that despite the goodwill of the support system, only a few organisations actively disseminated information about the services on offer to male victims of violence. As we have shown in Chap. 3, few people know that family protection also offers help to men who are experiencing violence in intimate relationships.

As mentioned before, most of the men in this study who have used a crisis centre report benefiting greatly from its services. This applies to both Norwegian and foreign men. A challenge that many men face in other parts of the system is that staff have not taken them seriously, have failed to recognise their role as fathers or have been suspicious of them. Seidler (1994) writes that men are educated to be careful about what they say because words can easily be used against them. As we have seen, the fathers in this part of the study spent a lot of time and thought finding strategies to avoid the switching of the violence relationship. A common strategy is not to talk about the violence to which they are being subjected.

For decades in Norway, there has been a strong political will to achieve gender equality. This has been expressed in the establishment of fathers' rights to paternity leave, and in proactively making moves to prevent violence and abuse against women. Norway is one of the countries in the world in which most women are in work or education, and where it is taken for granted in most areas of society that both parents will participate in the care and education of their children. The men we interviewed who have children express a strong desire to be actively involved as fathers. The majority have taken a long paternity leave and say they have taken considerable responsibility for housework and care of the children. As we have seen, we also have some dramatic examples of fathers who have been deprived of the opportunity to be a significant caregiver to their children. Our sample consists of modern fathers who are the main breadwinners and also victims of violence. Their stories have been silent thus far in the discourse about violence in intimate relationships. Gender-biased understandings in and outside the support agencies (who should ideally be helping children and both parents) can contribute to those agencies becoming co-agents in the reproduction of a stereotypical gendered bias about violence in close relationships.

Violence and abuse have major health, social and socio-economic consequences. Violence between parents also affects any children involved. We see the current emphasis on putting resources into the prevention of violence and abuse (including bullying), with a focus on children and young people, as extremely positive. Our study shows that men who were victims of sexual abuse at a young age also experienced physical and mental violence, neglect and, interestingly, bullying at school. With early detection of violence and abuse, and specific intervention and treatment where necessary, a great deal of human suffering can be reduced. We have seen in the Norwegian survey (Chap. 3) that even in the various official support systems whose mandate it is to offer support and help, there is a lack of knowledge about the services available for men who are being subjected to violence and abuse. We also know that several other countries in Europe and the Nordic regions do not have crisis centres or other emergency facilities for men who are experiencing serious violence in intimate relationships.

The Norwegian government's plan against violence and abuse for the period 2016–2021—*Opptrappingsplan mot Vold og overgrep* (Prop. 2016–2017)—provides an overview of possible measures to combat violence in close relationships, as well as violence and abuse against children, and of the main challenges related to the subject. The plan contains both short-term and long-term strategies to meet these challenges and presents a clear understanding of the major health and social consequences of violence and abuse.

Violence and abuse often lead to major physical and psychological problems for those individuals affected, and can also lead to lower educational attainment in school among children and adolescents, and thus poorer career opportunities later in life. For some, the consequences will be a reduced opportunity to participate in working life and a generally lower quality of life. The socio-economic costs, as pointed out in Prop. 2016–2017, are also significant.

The ambition behind this plan is to raise awareness and improve understanding among the wider public, but also to emphasise that the competence to deal with violence and abuse among professional groups appointed to do so (e.g. doctors, nurses, psychologists, police, lawyers) or those whose work puts them in a position to detect suspicious cases (e.g. teachers, staff working in child welfare) is worthwhile and valuable. The interviews with male victims of violence and abuse in our study indicate that such awareness is often lacking or entirely absent. Occasionally the lack of knowledge among various professionals has surfaced in shocking ways. Other studies have also found that discourses of masculinity and partner abuse frequently disadvantage men in identifying partner violence and seeking help (Corbally 2015).

It is crucial to identify violence early in order to prevent revictimisation. Victims of violence must be offered assistance. The public should be aware of the help available. Taken as a whole, our study provides the basis for the following general recommendations to prevent, detect and deal with violence in intimate relationships in Norway and in other countries:

- Preventative work is important, because violence and abuse have major health, social and societal consequences.
- Services offering help for men exposed to violence in intimate relationships (and their children) must be strengthened.
- Assistance for men subjected to violence in intimate relationships (and their children) must be better known about by the general public, by the victims of violence and in the support system itself.
- Understanding of issues that particularly affect men must be improved, including fear of and/or switching of the power/violence relationship and the threat of being deprived of parental care and contact with children.
- Psychological violence must be put on the agenda as a major offence against men, so that support agencies can detect violence against men more efficiently and offer adequate help and treatment.
- Awareness should be raised of the fact that psychological violence has serious consequences for the vulnerable.
- There is a need to strengthen the competence of general and specialist health services and mental health-care services in identifying and handling violence and sexual abuse against boys and men.

References

Bourdieu, P. (2001). *Masculine Domination*. Cambridge: Polity.

Bourdieu, P., & Passeron, J. (1977). *Reproduction in Education, Society and Culture* (Vol. 5, Sage studies in Social and Educational Change). London: Sage.

Coker, A. L., Davis, K. E., Arias, I., Desai, S., Sanderson, M., Brandt, H. M., & Smith, P. H. (2002). Physical and Mental Health Effects of Intimate Partner Violence for Men and Women. *American Journal of Preventive Medicine, 23*(4), 260–268.

Corbally, M. (2015). Accounting for Intimate Partner Violence. *Journal of Interpersonal Violence, 30*(17), 3112–3132.

Douglas, E. M., Hines, D. A., & McCarthy, S. C. (2012). Men Who Sustain Female-to-Male Partner Violence: Factors Associated with Where They Seek Help and How They Rate Those Resources. (Report) (Author abstract). *Violence and Victims, 27*(6), 871–894.

Felitti, V. J. (2003). The Origins of Addiction: Evidence from the Adverse Childhood Experience Study [Article in German]. *Prax Kinderpsychol Kinderpsychiatr, 52*(8), 547–559.

Felitti, V. J., Anda, R., Nordenberg, D., Williamssom, D., et al. (1998). Relationship of Child Abuse and the Household Dysfunction to Many of the Leading Causes of Death in Adults. The Adverse Childhood Experience Study. *American Journal of Preventive Medicine 1998, 14*(4), 245–258.

Gottzén, L. (2016). Displaying Shame: Men's Violence Towards Women in a Culture of Gender Equality. In *Response Based Approaches to the Study of Interpersonal Violence* (pp. 156–175). London: Palgrave Macmillan.

Grøvdal, Y., Jonassen, W., & Nasjonalt kunnskapssenter om vold og traumatisk stress (The Norwegian Centre for Violence and Traumatic Stress Studies). (2015). *Menn på krisesenter (Men at Crisis Centres)* (Vol. 5/2015, Report (Nasjonalt kunnskapssenter om vold og traumatisk stress: trykt utg.)) (The Norwegian Centre for Violence and Traumatic Stress Studies). Oslo: Nasjonalt kunnskapssenter om vold og traumatisk stress (The Norwegian Centre for Violence and Traumatic Stress Studies). Retrieved from https://www.nkvts.no/rapport/menn-pa-krisesenter/.

Haaland, T., Clausen, S., & Schei, B. (2005). *Vold i parforhold—ulike perspektiver: Resultater fra den første landsdekkende undersøkelsen i Norge (Violence in Partner Relationships—Various Perspectives: Results from the First Nationwide Survey in Norway)* (Vol. 2005:3, NIBR-report Oslo: Norsk institutt for by- og regionforskning (Norwegian Institute for Urban and Regional Research). Retrieved from http://www.hioa.no/Om-HiOA/Senter-for-velferds-og-arbeidslivsforskning/NIBR/Publikasjoner/Publikasjoner-norsk/Vold-i-parforhold-ulike-perspektiver.

Helweg-Larsen, K., & Frederiksen, M. L. (2008). *Vold mod maend i Danmark. Omfang og karakter (Violence Against Men in Denmark—Extent and Nature).* Minister for Equality, Statens Inst. for Folkesundhed (The National Institute of Public Health); Syddansk Universitet.

Hines, D. A., & Douglas, E. M. (2011). Symptoms of Posttraumatic Stress Disorder in Men Who Sustain Intimate Partner Violence: A Study of Helpseeking and Community Samples. *Psychology of Men & Masculinity, 12*(2), 112–127.

Hines, D., & Douglas, E. M. (2015). Health Problems of Partner Violence Victims: Comparing Help-Seeking Men to a Population-Based Sample. *American Journal of Preventive Medicine, 48*(2), 136–144.

Hines, D., Malley-Morrison, K., & Lisak, D. (2001). Psychological Effects of Partner Abuse Against Men: A Neglected Research Area. *Psychology of Men & Masculinity, 2*(2), 75–85.

Kimmel, M. (2002). "Gender Symmetry" in Domestic Violence. *Violence Against Women, 8*(11), 1332–1363.

Lopez, G., & Minoritetsperspektiver på norsk familievern—bidrag til et kultur-sensitivt familievern. (2007). *Minoritetsperspektiver på norsk familievern: Klienters erfaringer fra møtet med familievernkontoret (Minority Perspectives on the Norwegian Family Protection: The Experiences of Clients in Their Encounter with Family Protection Services)* (Vol. 9/07, NOVA-report. Oslo: Norsk insti-tutt for forskning om oppvekst, velferd og aldring.

Machado, A., Hincs, D., & Matos, M. (2016). Help-Seeking and Needs of Male Victims of Intimate Partner Violence in Portugal. *Psychology of Men & Masculinity, 17*(3), 255–264.

Seidler, V. (1994). *Unreasonable Men: Masculinity and Social Theory (Male Orders)*. London: Routledge.

Seidler, V. (1997). *Man Enough: Embodying Masculinities*. London: Sage.

Sogn, Hjemdal, & Hjemdal, Ole K. (2009). *Vold mot menn i nære relasjoner: Kunnskapsgjennomgang og rapport fra et pilotprosjekt (Violence Against Men in Intimate Relationships: A Review of Current Knowledge and Report from a Pilot Project)*. Oslo: Norsk kunnskapssenter om vold og traumatisk stress (NKVTS) (The Norwegian Centre for Violence and Traumatic Stress Studies). Retrieved from https://www.nkvts.no/rapport/vold-mot-menn-i-naere-relasjoner/.

The Norwegian Government's Plan Against Violence and Abuse for the Period 2016–2021. Opptrappingsplan for vold og overgrep (2017–2021) Prop. nr.12.S (2016–2017). Retrieved from https://www.regjeringen.no/conten-tassets/f53d8d6717d84613b9f0fc87deab516f/no/pdfs/prp201620170012000 dddpdfs.pdf.

Tjaden, P., Thoennes, N., Centers for Disease Control Prevention, & National Institute of Justice. (2000). *Full Report of the Prevalence, Incidence, and Consequences of Violence Against Women: Findings from the National Violence Against Women Survey*. U.S. Department of Justice, Office of Justice Programs, National Institute of Justice.

Open Access This chapter is licensed under the terms of the Creative Commons Attribution 4.0 International License (http://creativecommons.org/licenses/by/4.0/), which permits use, sharing, adaptation, distribution and reproduction in any medium or format, as long as you give appropriate credit to the original author(s) and the source, provide a link to the Creative Commons licence and indicate if changes were made.

The images or other third party material in this chapter are included in the chapter's Creative Commons licence, unless indicated otherwise in a credit line to the material. If material is not included in the chapter's Creative Commons licence and your intended use is not permitted by statutory regulation or exceeds the permitted use, you will need to obtain permission directly from the copyright holder.

8

The Need to Develop the Established Theory of Partner Violence Further

We started this book by showing that, in line with recent research, we would use Johnson's typology of violence in intimate relationships; that is, the divide between intimate terrorism and situational violence. We find that the violence perpetrated against the men we have interviewed must in the main be characterised as intimate terrorism. This is by no means surprising. Johnson points out that situational violence is largely revealed through population surveys, while intimate terrorism is identified through qualitative studies of particular groups exposed to violence. The reason for this is the significant difference between the extent of situational violence and intimacy terrorism detected through prevalence studies. As we have seen in the review of Nordic surveys in Chap. 2, the gender differences seem relatively small in the case of milder forms of physical partner violence, and several studies show that both men and women are both frequently subjected to control and abuse in partner relationships. We want to focus now, therefore, on intimate terrorism, and only to touch on situational violence.

A central premise for Johnson's concept of intimate terrorism is, as mentioned earlier, an asymmetric power relationship. In all relationships where there is serious and systematic violence, there will be a dominant

© The Author(s) 2019
M. I. Lien, J. Lorentzen, *Men's Experiences of Violence in Intimate Relationships*,
Palgrave Studies in Victims and Victimology,
https://doi.org/10.1007/978-3-030-03994-3_8

party. Feminist-oriented scholars have had a vast influence over the research about family violence and have contributed to highlighting women's and children's experiences of serious violence in intimate relationships. Johnson's theoretical perspective on gender and power has had a major impact on the analysis of clinical trials of abused women. Implicit to Johnson's perspective on intimate terrorism is his theory on gender power, which has its basis in the idea that men as a group dominate women as a group, and that systematic physical violence and control are motivated by the desire for dominance and oppression (Johnson 2008). Over the last decade there has been a cultural shift that has led research communities to recognise that men can be subjected to serious and systematic violence from both women and other men.

One reason for disagreement among partner violence researchers is the lack of clarity about what actually constitutes intimate terrorism. If one emphasises the aspect of control, as Johnson does, then any little slap or push could be considered intimate terrorism, as long as we find that the woman exercises control in a relationship. In that case, the number of male and female perpetrators will necessarily be equal. If the emphasis is placed on more systematic and long-term threatening behaviour and serious violence, which may include psychological, physical and sexual violence, the number of victims of violence will be fewer and we will approach what we might more intuitively understand by the term intimate terrorism.

An understanding of partner violence as a phenomenon which was originally based on the experiences of abused women with violent men, and founded on the understanding of a patriarchal society, must now be developed further to throw light on the serious and systematic psychological and physical partner violence perpetrated against men (see also Bell and Naugle 2008), since partner violence can be committed by both men and women (Simmons et al. 2014). Intimate terrorism can be exercised without the partner having physical superiority.

We find men who are in a privileged economic position and who are physically superior, who are nonetheless exposed to serious acts of violence. These events lead to feelings of worthlessness and suicidal ideation in these men. As shown in Chaps. 4 and 5, in such relationships it is not the partner who is physically superior (the man) who dominates, but the woman who exercises psychological control over the man. This book's primary contribution to the international debate on violence in intimate relationships lies perhaps in the fact that we have been able to clearly document the impact of psychological violence against men—what it comprises and how it is experienced. This must also have an impact on our wider understanding of what intimate terrorism entails.

Our research also shows a marked trend that those women who perpetrate violence often have psychological problems and have been both victims and perpetrators. There are strong indications that these women are in need of therapeutic treatment. As mentioned previously, studies of male perpetrators of violence in intimate relationships have shown that six out of ten men undergoing therapy have experienced childhood violence themselves and have major problems with anxiety, depression and substance abuse (Rangul Askeland et al. 2011). In a Norwegian interview study of mothers who inflicted violence on their children, Kruse and Bergman (2014) found that the mothers themselves had had earlier experiences of violence and had also subjected a partner or ex-partner to violence. These women say that the violence often occurred when they found the demands of looking after the children overwhelming. This reflects findings in the international literature on maternal violence (see Kruse and Bergman 2014) and challenges Johnson's (2008) sociological perspective on partner violence, showing the need to supplement it with other theoretical perspectives (see also Bell and Naugle 2008).

In several prevalence studies, Johnson's theory of men's need for dominance over women is used to explain why women are more vulnerable to domestic violence (Dobash and Dobash 1995, 2004; Kimmel 2002). We find it problematic to take the motive behind the violence for granted. Since we have not interviewed the wives and girlfriends (perpetrators) of the men in our survey, we can say nothing about their desire or need to control these men. Future studies should make it a priority to investigate women's motives for exercising violence in the family and to shed light on their experiences. What we can say here is that the men's experiences of being isolated and exposed to this form of violence over long periods erode their self-esteem, their desire to live and their sense of worth.

The psychological violence to which men are subjected, in the form of degradation as fathers, ridicule and humiliation, is not measured in several of the major investigations into violence. The most recent and most important survey in Norway investigating violence in intimate relationships does not include any questions about psychological violence (Thoresen and Hjemdal 2014). This necessarily means that the study fails to offer an adequate picture of the extent of violence against men in intimate relationships.

Both family protection and the crisis centre movement in Norway have been dominated by a biased focus on men's violence against women, which has in part been supported by previous feminist studies and the focus of Johnson and other feminist researchers on men's violence. There is reason to assume that a gender bias in samples and in empirical foundations has hindered the furtherance of knowledge about men's vulnerability and need for help (Douglas and Hines 2011; Fjell 2013; Schei and Bakketeig 2007; Grøvdal and Jonassen 2015).

Our study shows that men are also subjected to systematic violence. We find that male victims need help, but that there is significant resistance which makes it difficult for them to seek and access it. This resistance lies within the men themselves, in the relevant organisations and in society, and clearly has its roots in the established discourse about perpetrators and victims of violence. Additionally, much of our theoretical understanding of violence in intimate relationships supports a one-sided focus on women as the vulnerable party. It is crucial that theories be reassessed if we are to extend our knowledge about, and change our attitudes to, violence against men.

Masculinities Studies of Male Violence

In traditional research into men, the focus has been on men as the perpetrators of violence, and substantially less on them as victims of violence (Connell 1987, 2005; Kimmel 2002, 2006). When, in the late 1980s and early 1990s, men's studies began to establish itself as an independent field, it was strongly influenced by the contemporaneous feminist criticism of patriarchal structures. Historically, women as a group had been oppressed by men, economically, socially and ideologically. When it came to the question of violence, it was presented as a fact that men were the instigators of most violence, both at a collective and social level as well as on an individual level. It is the violence on an individual level that impacts many women and children. Men's violence towards, and general suppression of, women was the dominant social pattern in most societies; a gender-based suppression was in existence. This meant that the question of power became central, even in the emerging feminist-inspired research into men. This was further reinforced by the fact that this research was often fused with Marxist criticism of the capitalist society. Here, gender relations were understood in the same way that Marxism understood the relationship between the social classes: just as the bourgeoisie in a capitalist society was seen to be oppressive and to possess greater resources than the working classes, so too was the relationship between men and women seen as one of oppressor and oppressed. This thinking is apparent in sociologist R. W. Connell's theory of dominant hegemonic masculinity, which remains the most influential theory in this field.

Connell (1987, 2005) challenges the tendency in early feminist research to observe and describe men as one unique and homogeneous group. Connell points out that there are significant variations between men's circumstances and attitudes, which require us to talk about masculinities in the plural (Connell 2005). There are, for example, groups of oppressed men whose access to economic and political resources is more restricted than that of more influential men. Other groups of men are marginalised and largely powerless, for instance because of their ethnicity or other reasons. However, Connell only sees this oppression or marginalisation in relation to other men—these men are never seen as oppressed or marginalised in relation to women (Connell 2005).

Despite the fact that Connell demonstrates that there are various types of masculinities in any given society, with varying access to power, influence and resources, he upholds the original feminist premise that men as a group are always oppressive to women. Certain men can of course oppress other men, make them victims of violence, exploit them economically or marginalise them, yet these male victims nonetheless occupy a superior position to women (Connell 2005). The inner logic of this theory makes it virtually impossible to see women as anything but subordinate to men, and as victims of men's power and violence.

Although Connell's relatively influential theory is largely used within the field of social science, the same logic has also influenced major sections of men's studies, including historical research on men (Rotundo 1993; Kimmel 2002, 2006; Tjeder 2003). Despite various attempts at offering greater nuance, the feminist gender-power perspective on male dominance and female subordination prevails.

The Need for Alternative Theoretical Perspectives

As Jennifer Lawson (2012) points out, we must now work to bridge gaps between the polarised theories of violence and gender. The field of research on violence is still largely shaped by a sociological gender-power perspective and an oppressed/oppressor model. Not only is this problematic in the understanding of women, it is also highly problematic in the understanding of men. Nor does the gender-power model make sense in the analysis of violence in gay relationships.

From a historical perspective, it easy to understand why theoretical analyses have emphasised men's power. This is also understandable from a global perspective. The problem is that it has closed the way for a more phenomenological and realistic understanding of violence in intimate relationships, where both men and women are perpetrators of violence and power. There is not just *one* truth about serious partner violence and there cannot therefore be *one* theory to explain it: neither the causes of violence nor the reasons why some people are exposed to serious and systematic violence in intimate relationships. There is good reason to question physical superiority as a "natural" explanation of systematic partner violence, and of the fear of (more) violence. An uncritical acceptance of the discourse about the female victim and the myth of the good mother can contribute to acceptance of the violence perpetrated by women and mothers in intimate relationships, but also to the concealment of the violence that exists in gay relationships.

Established narratives of partner violence set limits on how men can talk about their experiences of violence. Foucault describes how discourses create "truth effects" (Foucault 1977). As we saw in the chapter on partner violence (Chap. 5), fathers feel that they must avoid bringing up the subject of women's violence in any discussion relating to children and their care, because they are afraid they might be suspected themselves. The accepted thinking within family protection appears to be characterised by the belief that the mother is best for the child and that men are perpetrators of partner violence, not the victims of it.

In Scandinavian men's studies, there has been a desire to show that many men in this part of the world have been positive in their attitude to more egalitarian relationships between the sexes; and that they have distanced themselves from the negative traits traditionally attached to the notion of manliness, such as violence or unwillingness to take responsibility for children and family (Holter 2007; Aarseth 2011). Using the concepts of unmanliness/manliness, some scholars have attempted to demonstrate the wide variations that characterise different forms of masculinity, where forms of manliness are almost always created and defined in direct relation to forms of unmanliness—which are marginalised and repudiated (Liliequist 1999; Andersson 2004; Lorentzen 2004; Ekenstam 2006; Lorentzen and Ekenstam 2006). Unmanliness, just like manliness, is dependent on historical context. At times unmanliness has been linked with a derisive view of femininity (Connell 1987; Kimmel 2002), but by no means always.

With this theoretical approach it has been possible to get closer to a more real and complex picture of manliness in all its diversity. This is a picture that shows vast differences in access to power and status among men, and recognises that many men are, or have been, subjected to oppression in similar ways to women. There was a desire to make clear the sense of emotional loss and powerlessness that exists in many ordinary men's lives. In several of the studies that look at the play between manliness and unmanliness, a need has been identified for a more phenomenological perspective; that is, we must listen to men's own voices and take their personal experiences seriously (Lorentzen 2004; Ekenstam 2006; Lorentzen and Ekenstam 2006).

Although we see that these attempts offer a more phenomenological picture of men's actual experiences, and of the variety and complexity that exist, we find, based on our present study, that this perspective has also been limited. Firstly, it seems from many of our interviews that some men who occupy the position of victim do not perceive themselves as unmanly, but on the contrary as manly. Secondly, it seems that it is not only other men, as previously believed, who define men as unmanly, but also the women with whom they have relationships. There is also the question of how important the matter of womanliness/manliness/unmanliness actually is to men's self-image, or, indeed, to our analysis of their relationships.

Some Problems with Structuralist Theory

A prominent voice in men's studies which has long criticised the biased focus on structural power relationships and the lack of a phenomenological perspective is that of sociologist Victor Seidler (1994, 1997, 2004). Seidler maintains that one problem with a structuralist theory is its universalism: it is a rationalist theory with generalisable claims. The variables are given beforehand, which means that many of the more self-contradictory features of reality are squeezed into overly narrow conceptual frameworks. In line with a western (generally masculine) scientific tradition, it reduces cultural variations, personal experiences and feelings to a minimum. Feelings such as grief, fear and vulnerability are acknowledged as little in this research as they are within the dominant male culture. This biased focus on structural relationships is even accompanied by the dismissal of what we can call the "personal", "emotional" or "therapeutic", particularly here, where power is presented as the most relevant question. Although there is a significant link between the concepts of manliness and power (and violence), manliness cannot always be reduced to power. As Ekenstam (2006) argues, the diversity of male identities, as well as the relationships between men and women, is too complex and the contradictions too many.

Seidler points out that an understanding of the power relationship between the genders, and the various social structures, must be the starting point of our analysis, not the end point. The biased structuralist approach to research on masculinity has meant that we actually know very little about how men think or perceive themselves. The neglect, abuse and violence they have experienced as children, as well as the disempowerment they may also have experienced, tend to be rendered invisible when masculinities are only seen in terms of power relationships. We lack insight into the fear, pain, suffering and sense of insecurity that many boys and men (also) experience throughout their lives.

Seidler believes it is necessary to develop new methods for interviewing men about their personal relationships. The researcher must be prepared to build a personal relationship and to allow men's own voices to be heard. It was just such an approach that inspired our work with this book.

In our study we have wanted to let the men tell their own stories and to allow their voices to come through. This study shows a complex picture of the violence to which men are subjected. Violence can be systematic over a period of time, it is psychological and physical, and it is threatening and dangerous. According to accounts given by the men who are experiencing partner violence, female perpetrators often (strategically) use society's assumption that men are assumed to be the violent partner. The challenge has been to meet these male voices with a theoretical understanding of the relationship between gender and family dynamics, and the relationship between each individual's history and their present situation.

In our interviews we talked to men about feelings of unmanliness associated with being exposed to violence, based on theories of unmanliness. We found, however, that men rarely define themselves as or see themselves as unmanly because they are victims of violence, or because they do not retaliate. On the contrary, many of them emphasise that they see it as an expression of manliness when they do *not* hit back. Additionally, both those who have/had male or female partners express that they had no intention or desire to use violence against their partner. This differs from the findings of several other interview studies, which have found that male victims of partner violence perceive themselves as unmanly (Bjerkeseth 2010; Morgan and Wells 2016).

Seidler (1994, 1997) criticizes structural perspectives that take their starting point in (male) physical and economic supremacy. Our study shows that men who are subjected to violence can in fact be socially and/or economically dominant, and that they see their strategy of non-violence as an expression of manliness. When, despite these factors, men are subjected to systematic violence, it seems obvious that a structural perspective is inadequate in seeking to understand violence towards men.

We need to include the dimension of *psychological dominance* if we are to explain psychological/physical violence against men. A position of psychological dominance is as easy for a woman to occupy as it is a man, and thus the analysis of violence will not be so strongly linked to the man. Such a theory will mean that gender itself will become less relevant to the understanding of violence in intimate relationships (see McHugh et al. 2013).

Our interviews show that these men have felt enormous caring and empathy for their partners. Despite being subjected to systematic and serious violence, they try to understand their violent partners and are concerned for the partners' care needs. These men find coping strategies in order to live with the violence, and for many of them this involves trivialising or under-communicating it. Meanwhile, some do not perceive themselves as being the victims of violence before a substantial amount of time has passed. One reason for this may be that men, like society and institutions in general, have internalised the understanding that women, not men, are exposed to violence. Thus, they lack the concepts for the violence to which they are exposed, until the violence has escalated to the point that it represents a real threat.

We suggest that new theoretical understandings of violence are urgently needed. Such a theorising must take into account the findings in this study. That is to say, it must be acknowledged that men also experience intimate terrorism in close relationships. One can no longer claim, as Johnson has done a number of times, that intimate terrorism is "almost exclusively" perpetrated by men. We have no basis on which to discuss the extent of violence towards men in comparison to the same form of violence towards women. Nor, perhaps, is this the most important factor in developing theoretical perspectives further. We need to adapt our research in order to get a better picture of the extent and nature of the intimate terrorism directed at men. A theoretical understanding that includes men who are exposed to serious violence necessarily implies that the traditional gender-power discourse must be modified and supplemented (see Bell and Naugle 2008). Violence in intimate relationships is a complex phenomenon that requires a variety of theoretical approaches (Bell and Naugle 2008; Lawson 2012). Perspectives and theoretical models must acknowledge that violence is perpetrated in same-sex relationships and by both sexes in heterosexual relationships; that ethnic background/nationality/residence status can further complicate matters; and finally that both the perpetrator's and the victim's personal histories are of importance. Our empirical findings also indicate that violence can have a basis in psychological dominance, and is therefore less linked to womanliness or manliness than previously thought. As we have touched upon, social backgrounds are relevant too in our understanding of people's vulnerability in a partner relationship.

Future Research on Violence in Intimate Relationships

Our study shows that there is a need for a more nuanced understanding of power relationships with regard to family violence, sexual abuse and intimate terrorism. It is not enough to investigate physical/economic superiority (structural power relationships) in order to understand violence in intimate relationships. As Russel Dobash and Emerson Dobash (2004) have pointed out, further research on violence in intimate relationships must include in-depth research about women's violence to male partners. We find that the structuralist understanding of violence must be supplemented with an understanding of how psychological dominance can provide a basis for power and coercion. As already outlined, it is necessary to have a new theoretical understanding of violence in intimate relationships which includes violence against men. Such an understanding implies that Johnson's concept of intimate terrorism also includes women's violence against men. Kimmel (2002) has suggested methods to reconcile the disparate data of gender symmetry and gender asymmetry, and encourages researchers and practitioners to acknowledge women's use of violence, while simultaneously understanding why this violence tends to be different from that perpetrated by men towards their female partners.

Our proposals for future research on violence in intimate relationships are as follows:

- Several larger qualitative studies of boys' and men's experiences and of how violence and sexual abuse in intimate relationships are handled.
- Closer investigation of the mechanisms behind men's silence on the subject of violence and abuse.
- Inclusion of gender and class perspectives in future studies.
- Method-development projects with the aim of improving the quality of research into violence against boys and men.
- Further studies that map the requirements of men for help and support.
- Future prevalence studies including questions that can throw light on various forms of psychological violence among adults.

References

Aarseth, H. (2011). *Moderne familieliv: Den likestilte familiens motivasjonsformer (Modern Family Life: Forms of Motivation in the Equality Based Family)*. Oslo: Cappelen Damm akademisk.

Andersson, S. (2004). Maktrelationer mellan män genom ålder. Status, auktoritet och marginalitet inom närpolisen (Power Relations Between Men Throughout Life. Status, Authority and Marginality in Local Policing. *Kvinnnovetenskaplig tidskrift*, nr 1–2. Retrieved from http://130.241.16.45/ojs/index.php/tgv/article/viewFile/2304/2058.

Bell, K. M., & Naugle, A. E. (2008). Intimate Partner Violence Theoretical Considerations: Moving Towards a Contextual Framework. *Clinical Psychology Review, 28*(7), 1096–1107.

Bjerkeseth, L. B. (2010). *Den Mannlige Offerrollen: En Intervjustudie Av Menn Som Opplever Vold Fra Kvinnelig Partner (The Male Victim: An Interview Study of Men Who Experience Violence by Female Partners)*. Master's dissertation, Department of Sociology and Social Geography at the University of Oslo. Retrieved from https://www.duo.uio.no/handle/10852/15305.

Connell, R. (1987). *Gender and Power: Society, the Person and Sexual Politics*. Cambridge: Polity Press.

Connell, R. (2005). *Masculinities* (2nd ed.). Berkley: University of California Press.

Dobash, R. P., & Dobash, R. E. (1995). Reflections on Findings from the Violence Against Women Survey. *Canadian Journal of Criminology, 37*(3), 457–304.

Dobash, R. P., & Dobash, R. E. (2004). Women's Violence to Men in Intimate Relationships: Working on a Puzzle. *British Journal of Criminology, 44*(3), 324–349.

Douglas, E., & Hines, D. (2011). The Helpseeking Experiences of Men Who Sustain Intimate Partner Violence: An Overlooked Population and Implications for Practice. *Journal of Family Violence, 26*(6), 473–485.

Ekenstam, C. (2006). The History and Future of Studies on Men and Masculinity: Some Theoretical Reflections. *Norma: Nordisk Tidsskrift for Maskulinitetsstudier (Nordic Journal for Masculinity Studies), 1*(1), 6.

Fjell, T. (2013). *Den usynliggjorte volden: Om menn som utsettes for partnervold fra kvinner (The Invisible Violence: About Men Subjected to Partner Violence from Women)*. Trondheim: Akademika.

Foucault, M. (1977). *Discipline and Punish: The Birth of the Prison*. New York: Pantheon Books.

Grøvdal, Y., Jonassen, W., & Nasjonalt kunnskapssenter om vold og traumatisk stress (The Norwegian Centre for Violence and Traumatic Stress Studies). (2015). *Menn på krisesenter (Men at Crisis Centres)* (Vol. 5/2015, Report (Nasjonalt kunnskapssenter om vold og traumatisk stress: trykt utg.)) (The Norwegian Centre for Violence and Traumatic Stress Studies). Oslo: Nasjonalt kunnskapssenter om vold og traumatisk stress (The Norwegian Centre for Violence and Traumatic Stress Studies). Retrieved from https://www.nkvts.no/rapport/menn-pa-krisesenter/.

Holter, Ø. (2007). *Män i rörelse: Jämställdhet, förändring och social innovation i Norden (Men in Motion: Gender Equality, Change and Social Innovation in the Nordic Region)*. Stockholm: Gidlund.

Johnson, M. P. (2008). *A Typology of Domestic Violence*. Boston: Northeastern University Press.

Kimmel, M. (2002). "Gender Symmetry" in Domestic Violence. *Violence Against Women, 8*(11), 1332–1363.

Kimmel, M. (2006). *Manhood in America: A Cultural History* (2nd ed.). New York: Oxford University Press.

Kruse, A., & Bergman, S. (2014). *"Jeg kan jo ikke kalle det noe annet enn vold-": En forskningsoversikt og en intervjustudie om mødres vold mot barn ("I Can't*

Call It Anything Else Than Violence": A Research Review and Interview Study of Mothers' Violence Against Children) (Vol. 4/2014, Report) Nasjonalt kunnskapssenter om vold og traumatisk stress (The Norwegian Centre for Violence and Traumatic Stress Studies). Oslo: Nasjonalt kunnskapssenter om vold og traumatisk stress. Retrieved from https://www.nkvts.no/rapport/jeg-kan-jo-ikke-kalle-det-noe-annet-enn-vold-en-forskningsoversikt-og-en-intervjustudie-om-modres-vold-mot-barn/.

Lawson, J. (2012). Sociological Theories of Intimate Partner Violence. *Journal of Human Behavior in the Social Environment, 22*(5), 572–590.

Liliequist, J. (1999). Från niding till sprätt. En studie i det svenska omanlighetsbegreppets historia från Vikingatid till sent 1700-tal *(From Caitiff to Weakling: A Study of the Concept of Unmanliness from Viking Times to the 18th Century)* In A-M Berggren *Manligt och omanligt i ett historiskt perspektiv (Manliness and Unmanliness in a Historical Perspective).* Stockholm, Forskningsrådsnämnden (Research Council), Report 99:4.

Lorentzen, J. (2004). *Maskulinitet: Blikk på mannen gjennom litteratur og film (Masculinity: Looking at Man Through Literature and Film).* Oslo: Spartacus.

Lorentzen, J., & Ekenstam, C. (2006). *Män i Norden: Manlighet och modernitet 1840–1940 (Man in the Nordic Regions: Manliness and Modernity).* Hedemora: Gidlund.

McHugh, M., Rakowski, C., & Swiderski, S. (2013). Men's Experience of Psychological Abuse: Conceptualization and Measurement Issues. *Sex Roles, 69*(3), 168–181.

Morgan, W., & Wells, M. (2016). 'It's Deemed Unmanly': Men's Experiences of Intimate Partner Violence (IPV). *The Journal of Forensic Psychiatry & Psychology, 27*(3), 1–15.

Rangul Askeland, I., Evang, A., & Heir, T. (2011). Association of Violence Against Partner and Former Victim Experiences: A Sample of Clients Voluntarily Attending Therapy. *Journal of Interpersonal Violence, 26*(6), 1095–1110.

Rotundo, E. (1993). *American Manhood: Transformations in Masculinity from the Revolution to the Modern Era.* New York: Basic.

Schei, B., & Bakketeig, L. S. (2007). *Kvinner lider—menn dør: Folkehelse i et kjønnsperspektiv (Women Suffer—Men Die: Public Health in a Gender Perspective).* Oslo: Gyldendal akademisk.

Seidler, V. (1994). *Unreasonable Men: Masculinity and Social Theory (Male Orders).* London: Routledge.

Seidler, V. (1997). *Man Enough: Embodying Masculinities.* London: Sage.

Seidler, V. J. (2004). Des/orienterade maskuliniteter. Kroppar, känslor och rädsla (Dis/orientated Masculinities. Bodies, Feelings and Fears. *Kvinnnovetenskaplig tidskrift* nr 1–2.

Simmons, J., Wijma, B., & Swahnberg, K. (2014). Associations and Experiences Observed for Family and Nonfamily Forms of Violent Behavior in Different Relational Contexts Among Swedish Men and Women. *Violence and Victims, 29*(1), 152–170.

Thoresen, S., & Hjemdal, O. K. (2014). *Vold og voldtekt i Norge: En nasjonal forekomststudie av vold i et livsløpsperspektiv (Violence and Rape in Norway: A National Prevalence Study of Violence in a Lifespan Perspective)* (Vol. 1/2014, Report (Nasjonalt kunnskapssenter om vold og traumatisk stress: trykt utg.)) (The Norwegian Centre for Violence and Traumatic Stress Studies). Oslo: Nasjonalt kunnskapssenter om vold og traumatisk stress (The Norwegian Centre for Violence and Traumatic Stress Studies). Retrieved from https://www.nkvts.no/rapport/vold-og-voldtekt-i-norge-en-nasjonal-forekomststudie-av-vold-i-et-livslopsperspektiv/.

Tjeder, D. (2003). *The Power of Character. Middle-Class Masculinities, 1800–1900*. Stockholm: Doctoral Thesis Monograph—University of Stockholm.

Open Access This chapter is licensed under the terms of the Creative Commons Attribution 4.0 International License (http://creativecommons.org/licenses/by/4.0/), which permits use, sharing, adaptation, distribution and reproduction in any medium or format, as long as you give appropriate credit to the original author(s) and the source, provide a link to the Creative Commons licence and indicate if changes were made.

The images or other third party material in this chapter are included in the chapter's Creative Commons licence, unless indicated otherwise in a credit line to the material. If material is not included in the chapter's Creative Commons licence and your intended use is not permitted by statutory regulation or exceeds the permitted use, you will need to obtain permission directly from the copyright holder.

Index

© The Author(s) 2019
M. I. Lien, J. Lorentzen, *Men's Experiences of Violence in Intimate Relationships*,
Palgrave Studies in Victims and Victimology,
https://doi.org/10.1007/978-3-030-03994-3